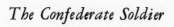

*The Confederate Soldier*

# The Confederate Soldier

by
## LeGrand James Wilson

*New Edition Edited by*

JAMES W. SILVER

*Foreword by Bell I. Wiley*

MEMPHIS STATE UNIVERSITY PRESS

Originally published in a small edition,
Fayetteville, Arkansas, 1902

Illustrated with original photographs ob-
tained from relatives and acquaintances
of LeGrand James Wilson.

Library of Congress Card Number 72-95936
ISBN: 0-87870-016-1

## Foreword

"I am not writing up a history of the war but . . . a history of the Confederate Soldier . . . as he was on the march, in the camp, in the ditches, on the battlefield." Thus did LeGrand James Wilson describe his objective in writing the reminiscences here reproduced.

Wilson was well qualified to accomplish the purpose to which he committed himself. His service as a line officer in the First Mississippi Volunteers and then as a surgeon in the Forty-second Mississippi Regiment brought him in close touch with the men in the ranks and enabled him to observe them under a variety of circumstances. His training as a physician enriched his understanding of human nature and enhanced his powers of observation. His narrative affords interesting insights into the life and character of the men who wore the gray and makes more understandable the brilliant achievements on the march and in combat of the ragged and poorly nourished Rebs who followed Lee, Longstreet and Jackson in the arduous campaigns of the American Civil War.

Wilson's account also gives revealing glimpses of Confederate medical practice. Since personal narratives of surgeons who served with the Southern forces are relatively rare, these comments on the care of the sick and wounded add much to the value of the book.

All in all this memoir is a substantial contribution to Confederate history.

BELL IRVIN WILEY
Emory University.

7

# Contents

# List of Illustrations

.

# Introduction

In May, 1901, LeGrand James Wilson, medical practitioner in Alma, Arkansas, came away from a Confederate reunion in Memphis with the determination "to write a history of the Confederate soldier, and attempt to show him as he was on the march, in the camp, in the ditches, on the battle-field, and I shall endeavor to pursue this plan to the end." This he proceeded to do, the resulting *Confederate Soldier* being published the following year in Fayetteville, Arkansas.

The sixty-five year old author wrote apparently from memory of his own experiences in the Confederate army more than thirty years before. Although he kept "a condensed school history" by his side so as not to go astray on dates and names, his story is not so much of battles and campaigns as of everyday life of the civilian soldier as viewed by a competent observer, an army surgeon. A keen judge of men, a reliable witness with a sense of humility and a delightful capacity for wit and understatement, Dr. Wilson recorded without fear, favor or rancor his impressions of the friends and neighbors who went off to defend their country through four heartbreaking years. Long out of print, *The Confederate Soldier* well merits the attention of those concerned with the human side of the war.

Exciting bits of Confederate drama range from Wilson's hairbreadth but casual escape through the Union lines from Fort Donelson, to the heart-breaking particulars of Gettysburg, and a doctor's ministrations to the maimed on that terrible retreat into Virginia. The war is examined in considerable measure from the medical side

13

—clinical discussions of treatment of the wounded on the battlefield, stories of dramatic deaths and recoveries, the almost universal accumulation of "childhood" diseases before the volunteers settled down to the business of being regulars, and ill-equipped and over-crowded hospitals. There is a great deal in this volume about the intricacies of travel in the Confederacy from 1861 to 1865, with Dr. Wilson testing the merits of local hostelries and sampling every mode of transportation from train and boat to hack, ambulance, and broken-down nag. Perhaps most intimately described is camp life, with its homesickness, recreation, religion, carousing, elections, and just plain ennui. The narrator tells of chance meetings with President Davis, General Lee, a Negro veteran of the War of 1812, and a Confederate spy named John. But he never departs long from his main theme, the story of the Confederate soldier from the moment of exuberance displayed at the organization of the local company until he returned to his family on foot or in a coffin—or was buried in an unmarked grave a thousand miles from home.

Fortunately, Dr. Wilson's excursion into writing did not stop with *The Confederate Soldier*. Three years later he published *The History of a Southern Presbyterian Family* which contains a great deal of information about his branch of the Wilson family as well as considerable insight into the personality of the author. It may be, as he claimed, that "there is so little change in a well-regulated Presbyterian family that the history of one child is the history of all." At least he was proud that there was "not a skeptic or infidel to be found" for a hundred years in this family of farmers, doctors, and educators. Strongly

14

Calvinistic, the Wilsons were likely to be well educated without going to college, neither rich nor poor, not ordained ministers but "preachers" in daily life. They were hardy, sober, industrious, well disciplined with a great sense of rectitude, and voted the Whig ticket as long as two parties existed in the South. "I never heard of one being sent to the hospital for any capital operation, to the blind or insane asylum, and but *one* to the State legislature," wrote their biographer. He did admit, with a degree of toleration, that an individual in the clan had a tendency toward hard drink, and that another who had turned Methodist "will do wrong sometimes . . . will practice 'falling from grace.' If he would only *believe* that horrible doctrine, and not practice it, no harm would be done."

*The History of a Southern Presbyterian Family* is dedicated to the descendants of Stephen Wilson, who came to Virginia from England about 1730, and of Dr. Nicholas Joseph Bourdon, a surgeon in the French navy who settled in Dinwiddie County, Virginia, at the close of the Revolution. Stephen's grandson James Wilson married Elizabeth Joseph Bourdon (the surgeon's daughter) in 1814 and two years later the young couple made the long trek from eastern Virginia to northern Alabama. To James and Elizabeth Wilson were born eleven children, including LeGrand James, named for an earlier brother who died at twelve of "pernicious malarial fever." In the winter of 1835-36 the Wilsons moved to Lincoln County, Tennessee, where LeGrand James came into the world on April 8, 1836.

The stay in Tennessee was not a long one for the family decided to try its fortune in northern Mississippi.

15

This journey required five weeks. The cavalcade, including forty slaves, 100 hogs, 20 cattle, and 40 turkeys, arrived in January, 1843, at the new farm home five miles northeast of Chulahoma. Already a roomy log house, gin house, stables, cotton press, and comfortable quarters for the Negroes were available and in the first season the Wilsons grew 48 bales of cotton on 60 rented acres. After two years of "looking around," James Wilson purchased near Chulahoma 640 acres which he apparently sold in the 1850's about the time of his acquisition of another large farm at Wall Hill.

Faithful Presbyterian that he was, James Wilson took a leading part in the building of the Chulahoma church. When division threatened the country, he "was uncompromising for the Union," but with the secession of Mississippi, he, also, "crossed the Rubicon." He was remembered by his son as "a kind husband and father and I never saw him correct one of his children but once, and I did not see much of that, but felt it." On May 1, 1861 Elizabeth Joseph Wilson died; her farmer-teacher husband lived another ten years.

LeGrand James Wilson, reared from childhood in Marshall County, attended Union Academy for four years, under the tutelage of the Reverend Samuel I. Reid, alumnus of Washington College, Pennsylvania. Mr. Reid was pastor, tutor, and friend of the family. The academy graduate taught school for five months while beginning the "reading" of medicine under his older brother, Dr. George A. Wilson, and Dr. William M. Compton. After two years of this, Wilson attended his first course of lectures at the University of Nashville before returning to Wall Hill to start medical practice in March, 1857. For eighteen months he was in contact, within eight miles of his office, with four established physicians who offered counsel "free of cost." In September, 1858, Wilson matriculated at Jefferson Medical College in Philadelphia where he passed an examination before returning to Mississippi in March, 1859.

On February 28, 1860 the young doctor married Elizabeth Carey Skipwith, a great-granddaughter of General Nathanael Greene. Though at the time the bride was from Memphis, the couple had been school mates (segregated by sex) at Union Academy. They settled down with his parents at Wall Hill, about sixty miles from Memphis—for a longer stay than either could have anticipated.

After Appomattox, Dr. Wilson's assets consisted of "a blind Canadian mare that the Yankee cavalry would not have." His first medical supplies were bought with the proceeds from a bale of cotton hidden by a friend from the rapacious invaders. On June 25, 1865 Wilson set up his medical office at Tyro, Mississippi, and six months later commenced his first housekeeping since marriage. Of seven children (Frank Small, James Compton, Bourdon, LeGrand James, Jr., Adrian Campbell, Clara Elizabeth, Peyton Rhea) only the last two were living at the turn of the century. In 1882 the Wilsons moved to Alma, Arkansas, where the author was living when he wrote *The Confederate Soldier*.

On the theory that "one pound of religion in the *home* is worth a bushel on the street corner," the Wilson family took the Bible as their "Magna Charta," teaching the children "reverence for God, and their parents, His holy word, and sanctuary." The father was not sure the

17

world was getting better,—"I am satisfied there is a great room for improvement." Christian people, he thought, "have got into a rush." His family life was exceptionally happy, a circumstance which he attributed to his wife, who was an excellent nurse, a good organist, a fine vocalist fond of Scottish ballads, and a constant reader— "my encyclopedia of general knowledge."

Dr. Wilson was a stout prohibitionist, a crusader against gambling and the desecration of the Sabbath. The stock market, he feared, cultivated a desire to get something for nothing; "It has not only become fashionable but the Devil has almost succeeded in making it respectable." As for Sunday, he wrote, "Every Christian living in and around Alma who visited the great World's Fair in St. Louis, started on a Saturday evening. By this means they saved a whole day. Will a man rob God? Again, look at the Sabbath evening buggy-riding of the young people of your town . . . a very dangerous practice."

After forty-five years of married life, when his wife had fifteen more years of life before her and he was to live yet another seven, Dr. Wilson recalled one of the favorite ballads of "the partner of my joys and sorrows":

> John Anderson, My Jo, John,
> We clamb the hill thegither,
> And mony a canty day, John,
> We've had wi'ane anither;
> Now we maun totter down, John,
> But hand in hand we'll go,
> And sleep thegither at the foot,
> John Anderson, my Jo!

*The Confederate Soldier* is reproduced as it appeared in 1902, with augmented title, with corrections of typographical errors and with the addition of a number of pictures. There was no index in the original. In only one instance has there been any serious change in the published work. Dr. Wilson's narrative stopped on page 177. After that came a sort of appendix of ten pages, an exhortation to the Confederate veteran of the turn of the century. The last veteran has passed away. The defense of southern action in 1860-61 as given by Dr. Wilson consists mainly of lengthy quotations from Chaplain-General Jones and President Davis and is familiar to all informed southerners. Inasmuch as these pages are somewhat extraneous and interfere with the continuity of a well told story, it has been decided to omit them from the present edition.

There has been no attempt to follow up all the ramifications of *The Confederate Soldier* but it is hoped that the footnotes will satisfy most of the questions arising in the mind of the general reader. The most fortunate "discovery" to help illumine some of the dark corners of Dr. Wilson's narrative was the diary of Major Robert W. Locke, a neighbor from Thyatira whose intimate friendship long outlasted the war—the two of them organized Company D of the 42nd Mississippi Regiment in 1862 and on May 14, 1865 they journeyed together to Grenada to obtain their paroles. This diary is now in the possession of Locke's granddaughter, Mrs. L. J. Wells, of Senatobia, Mississippi, who has generously allowed the use of some family pictures. Two grandnephews of Dr. Wilson, Alfred H. Holden, Germantown, Tennessee, and John A. Holden, Milwaukee, Wisconsin, have displayed from the beginning an unflagging concern in the re-issue of *The Confederate Soldier* and have contributed valuable documents and information. Frances Jane Barlow, William Collins, Nancy Jane Ramsey, and Carol Lindsey Spight, students in History 520 at the University of Mississippi, have gathered many of the details appearing in the footnotes. The late Dorothy Oldham, curator of the Mississippi Collection at the University of Mississippi Library, and Charlotte Capers and Mrs. Carl Black, Jr., of the Mississippi Department of Archives and History in Jackson have been extremely helpful.

JAMES W. SILVER
University of South Florida

# Leaving Home

I will describe in this chapter as best I can, the hardest battle ever fought by a Confederate soldier, a battle in which we all took a hand, and as far as I know, acted with becoming bravery, and survived the fight. I allude to the battle of leaving home, bidding farewell to all we hold dear—father, mother, wife and little ones. Gettysburg, Chickamauga and Shiloh were pretty tough places, but I believe that this was the hardest struggle of the war!

I shall never forget the 9th day of July, 1861. My company[1] was ordered to meet at Wall Hill,[2] a village in the western part of Marshall county, Miss., to start to Iuka, Miss., to be equipped, drilled and prepared for service. The 8th was a busy day at my father's, and a hundred other homes in the surrounding country, getting everything ready for the young soldiers.

We were ordered to carry a week's rations from home. A ham must be boiled, bread baked, a quantity of coffee parched and ground, sugar, preserves, pickles, cakes, et al., a large box full was prepared; and my father[3] had a barrel of kraut made that the boys might have some vegetable food while in camp, for we expected to remain in Iuka about two months. My young wife[4] insisted that I should take her nice sole leather trunk (a wedding present), and she packed it with all my best clothes, a fine pair of shoes, embroidered pair of slippers, comb, brush, toilet articles and shaving apparatus. They would not allow me to make any suggestions or have anything to do in the premises. My old Nurse Rose rolled up a lounge feather bed, blankets, pillows, etc., and I really had more baggage than the entire company possessed six months later on. I looked on, but said little as these preparations were made, with a strange feeling about my vest.

I followed my wife around with my little boy[5] in my arms, who seemed unusually attractive, and seemed to understand that something unusual was going on. And as the preparations were nearly completed, and night drew on, a peculiar sensation of sadness and quiet seemed to settle down upon the household. This last night at home! Would it really be the last? When I look into their eyes on the morrow, shall I see them no more in this life?

Night passed away, morning came, and after breakfast all were called in to prayers. My dear old father 70 years of age, read the 90th Psalm[6] and tried to pray. I know that prayer was partly answered, for I am still here. Shaking hands with the servants, we rode over to Wall Hill, where we met the entire neighborhood—fathers, mothers, wives, children, sweethearts and all. The little village of Wall Hill never witnessed such a scene, or had such a crowd before or since.

Old Capt. Milam,[7] a veteran of the Mexican war, rode up at 10 o'clock, and we knew we would soon have to start. An awful silence fell upon the whole crowd. Both parties seemed to be summoning all their strength and patriotism for the final moment. Provision had been made for all to ride in wagons, buggies, etc., to Holly

Springs, and at 10:30 the command was given—"Fall in Men!" But not one man fell into line. Again and again the command was given with no better results. At 11 o'clock Capt. Milam drew his sword, waved it over his head, and in a choking voice cried: "Boys, I'm going, will you follow me?" and started down the road. It must be done—the last kiss, the last embrace, the last clasp of the hand—the boys are gone, the battle won, a victory gained.

We reached Holly Springs before night, and the citizens carried us to their homes for supper. Next morning quite a crowd of ladies and gentlemen collected at the depot to see the company off, and I expected another sad scene, but as this train stopped the city band struck up Dixie, and every boy scrambled upon the cars, waving his hat and yelling like a veritable rebel.

Isn't it strange the effect Dixie had upon us in the long ago? Isn't it strange the effect it has upon us in our old age? We reached Iuka about 5 p.m. No preparations had been made for us. The General conducted us out to the camping place about one mile from town, and told us to make ourselves as comfortable as possible, that our tents and camp equipage would be up on the next train. We managed by hiring a couple of wagons from the country, and carrying a good deal on our shoulders, to get all our baggage out before night except my barrel of kraut, which was left upon the platform, there being no depot in which to store it. The next train was a long time coming, for it was the evening of the fourth day before our camping outfit arrived.

In the meantime we had a regular July rain and thunder storm, which did not add much to our comfort, but we had to learn to be soldiers, and we stood it like little men. It was amusing to see the men sheltering themselves. They were afraid to take advantage of a tree on account of the lightning, hence bushes were in demand. A few of the boys had umbrellas, and each was out in an open space and had a half dozen occupants.

As soon as we got the camp arranged and tents up, I went for my barrel of kraut. We were getting tired of cold rations and we needed a change, and we thought the kraut would prove to be a good thing. I started for it early in the morning, that we might enjoy it at dinner. As I drew near the corner of the street before turning to the depot, I met a man holding his nose and in a run, and just before meeting me he turned loose his nose, exclaiming; "Golly, what a stink!" "What's the matter friend?" "Go on," he said, "and you will find out." Another came round the corner, and as he turned loose his proboscis, he exclaimed bitterly: "D—n the man that brought that cabbage to town!" I didn't take the hint, but as I turned the corner the hint struck me full in the face. What a sight! The hot July sun had caused my kraut to ferment and burst the barrel, and it was foaming and fizzing, swelling and smelling. There was more cabbage than could have been crammed in half dozen barrels with a compress, and such a stench! I never smelt anything to compare to it. I never claimed that cabbage.

# *Organizing the First Mississippi Regiment*

In writing up my own history and adventures, I am compelled to write to a certain extent the history of the 1st Mississippi Regiment,[1] and I do this with a great deal of pleasure, and feel like I am discharging a duty, to relate what little I know of this gallant regiment, because I have never seen anything in print in regard to the part they acted in the great drama. Probably because so few of them survived the great struggle, possibly because their history was a very sad one.

Nearly one half of the war was spent by this regiment in prison, and if I remember correctly, a large percentage of the gallant men and officers who left the State in 1861, sleep around Camp Chase[2] and on Johnson's Island.[3] I can at least write their history up to the point of separation at Fort Donelson. Their "prison life," thank God, I know nothing of, so I continue my story. The companies came. in rapidly, and in less than a week twenty were on the ground ready to be formed into regiments. An order was sent out by the General for ten companies to be known as the 1st Mississippi Regiment, to appoint Judges, etc., and on the morrow to hold an election for field officers— one Colonel, one Lieut. Colonel and one Major.

This election proved to be an exciting one, so many of the company officers aspired to higher positions, and their election would cause vacancies in the companies, which would have to be filled. So many men as well as officers had a chance for promotion, hence the interest and excitement rapidly developed, and there was any amount of electioneering and canvassing going on until late at night among men and officers.

Capt. John M. Simonton[4] was elected Colonel on the first ballot. He was from the eastern part of the State, and was a fine specimen of manhood, tall, handsome, and as straight as an Indian, of commanding appearance and fine voice. This proved to be a wise selection, for Col. Simonton made a most excellent officer, and was greatly loved and respected by the entire regiment from first to last.

Balloting for Lieutenant Colonel created increased excitement and interest, as there were several candidates, and the most prominent aspirants being from the eastern portion of the State, this aroused considerable sectional feeling, and produced fuel for increased electioneering and canvassing. After several ballots the East prevailed, and Capt. [A. S.] Hamilton[5] received the majority, and was declared elected.

Col. H. was a small man, quick in his movements and nervous and excitable. He was a Methodist preacher of considerable ability, and made a most excellent drill offi-cer, and had the strongest and most powerful voice I ever heard. He loved to drill the men in skirmish tactics, and the men declared they could hear his commands when he was a half mile in their rear, and that he could see their mistakes when he was out of sight; that he "cussed them all the week, and preached and prayed for them all day Sunday." Grief and mortification at the surrender of Fort Donelson brought on an acute mania, which killed him a

26

short time after reaching prison on Johnson's Island.

The election of Major produced intense excitement. Office seekers increased, and it began to look like the eastern part of the State would get all of the field officers. One or two who had received a handsome vote for Lieut. Colonel, made the mistake of announcing themselves candidates for Major. This really looked like office seeking, and produced quite a sensation. The privates, too, began to think they were doing the most of the voting, and were certainly entitled to some of the spoils. Pretty soon some man stepped out, and in a ringing voice nominated "Tom Johnston,[6] private in Capt. Boone's company,[7] from DeSoto county, candidate for Major." It was a bold stroke. Up to this time the fight had been between the Captains of the regiment, and this the first and only private who had been proposed. They had been entirely overlooked in the excitement. The idea spread rapidly from man to man, and presently Tom Johnston was called from a dozen different points on the campus, which soon became one continuous shout for Tom Johnston. This brought a modest, rather effeminate young man to the front, who, in a tremulous voice, and quivering with excitement, made a pretty little war speech and the fight was won. The ballots were taken and Tom Johnston swept the field from end to end. Maj. Johnston was a success, and was always a favorite with the men, who felt that he was nearer to them than either of the other officers. I never heard him accused of but one fault by his men, a criminal carelessness of his own person on the battle field. This may have been imaginary on the part of the men, but it shows their love for their Major. The whole day was taken up in this exciting election, and the men went to their tents perfectly satisfied, but there were sore headed officers for weeks to come.

The next day the camp was regularly arranged, a guard detailed and placed on duty, and the General's first order was read on dress parade. This order caused a storm in camp. The particular brick which broke the camel's back was this: "No soldier shall leave camp or visit Iuka except on pass signed by company and regimental officers, and approved by the Brigadier General commanding." The idea of asking for a pass was something new and unexpected to the young soldier. The idea of carrying a pass was repugnant to an American freeman's feelings of honor, contrary to the teachings of the "declaration of independence," and a little more than a Calhoun county democrat could stand, and amusing expressions and very ugly expressions were heard in certain quarters long after "dress parade." We retired sooner than usual that evening, as we were worn out with the excitement of the day. After we had been asleep for some time, we were aroused from our slumbers by Capt. B.,[8] of Company F, who said he was in trouble, and wanted Capt. Milam. Capt. B. said that his men were in line, and swore they were going home, that they wouldn't stand such orders as were read that evening, and that they would not be influenced by anything he could say to them, but he believed they would listen to an old man.

Capt. Milam went with him, and succeeded in quieting the men by telling them to wait a day, and he would see Gen. [James Lusk] Alcorn,[9] and get him to revoke the order or modify it, so a democrat could comply with its demands. The next evening Gen. Alcorn rode out on his fine horse dressed in full uniform, had the regiments formed in hollow square, and made them a speech.

He instructed them in the duties of a soldier, he never alluded to the trouble of the previous night; he told them they had volunteered of their own free will and belonged to their country, and the country expected every man to do his duty; that they were now in a school of instruction, and must submit to military authority and discipline to become soldiers. Gen. Alcorn made a fine patriotic speech, and we had no more trouble, and quietly settled down to the duties of camp life, drilling four hours each day, and the officers studying Hardee's Tactics[10] about twelve. So our military education progressed.

# III

## Camp Life

―――――◄◆►―――――

Camp life grows monotonous in a short time. The novelty soon wears off, and its routine duties become tiresome indeed. We were in camp during July and August. Reveille at 5 a.m., roll call; breakfast 7; surgeon's call, 8; guard mounting 9; squad drill or drilling in the manual of arms to 10; company drill to 11; recess—dinner 12m. From 2 to 4, company and regimental drill, which generally was prolonged to 5; dress parade 6; supper 7; taps 9. Thus the days came and went, and our military education progressed.

Signs of an epidemic of nostalgia soon made its appearance, and required active treatment. The introduction of games and sports for the men became imperative, and cards, checkers, chess and marbles were soon introduced, but marbles proved to be the popular game, and a good taw was worth its weight in silver.

During the fifth week letters from home brought the pleasant intelligence that the good people held a mass meeting at Wall Hill for the benefit of the Alcorn Rifles, and readily made up a purse of $2,000 to purchase uniforms for the company. This indeed, was pleasant news, good news for the boys. It showed that the dear ones at home were "thinking" about us, and studying our welfare. It was a pleasant reminder, and had more effect in dispelling the blues than all the games. They knew that the

State of Mississippi nor our dear little Confederacy had Quartermaster's supplies for her soldiers; and as we expected to be ordered north into Kentucky, by the time the goods could be purchased and made up, cold weather would be coming on, and we would really be in need of heavier clothing. God bless the home folks.

We were requested at once to send home our measures as a committee of ladies and merchants had gone to Memphis to purchase the goods. Luckily we found a tailor in the regiment, and had him detailed to measure the men, which was accomplished, and the measures sent home.

Rumors of marching orders began to be circulated in camp occasionally, and sure enough about September 1st orders came to pack up, strike tents at 5 o'clock, cook two days rations, and be ready to take the 5 o'clock east bound train next evening. This order read on dress parade, caused possibly more excitement in camp than the first in regard to passes and camp discipline. Many letters must be written home. Every man must write, and most of the boys had more than one letter to write, and it must be done tonight, so no attention was paid to taps, and candles were burning long after midnight.

Some one must be sent back for those uniforms and Quartermaster's stores. Who would be the lucky man? That was thirty-nine years ago (old comrade) and I don't know how the question was decided, but I do know that the writer received the appointment, and as the boys boarded the east-bound train for Bowling Green, Kentucky, I started west for home, the happiest man in the regiment, and reached Holly Springs at 9 o'clock that night. Securing a buggy and driver, I was soon on my way to the old homestead, eighteen miles west.

31

I still remember how eager I was to get on; how slow the horse seemed to travel, how often I admonished my driver to whip up. Slow or fast, a few minutes after 12 we turned into the lawn leading up to my father's house, the dearest spot on earth to me. Desiring to slip in and not disturb my old father, and to surprise my wife, I drove around to the quarters to call one of the servants to look after the horse and driver, but when I reached the first door, and knocking called "Nelson," my old nurse Rose knew my voice, and rushed out yelling like a Comanche: "Thar's Mars. Jim! Thar's Mars. Jim! I tole Miss Betty he was coming. I knowed he'd be home tonight!" and roused the whole camp, and before I could shake hands, give orders and reach the back door, Miss Betty and the old Patriarch were there to meet me. Home again! Good night!

Next morning we rode over to Brock's Chapel,[1] where we had been accustomed for years to meet with God's people to worship. Now it was changed into a military workshop to manufacture clothing for Confederate soldiers. Six sewing machines occupied the altar. Two tables were erected upon the pews for the tailor who had volunteered to cut the clothing, and assist the ladies in making it up. The whole audience of twenty-five or more mothers, wives and daughters were busy at work. When I walked into the dear old church, machines suddenly stopped, and a dozen cried out:

"Where are the boys, Lieutenant?"

They knew what my coming meant. They knew the boys had gone to the front. I had to talk to every one, and answered a thousand questions to parents, wives and sweethearts, and this continued for a week, for a new set

32

of hands came every morning to work, and the time passed rapidly and pleasantly. When the day for packing arrived, I was astonished at the amount of work accomplished, and the quantity of clothing the good people had prepared for "the boys," as they loved to call them.

As I was present and assisted in packing, I remember something of the quantity: 102 suits complete, grey uniforms, 400 shirts, 200 pair of drawers, 500 pairs home knit woolen socks, besides a host of extra articles for soldiers I might find in need, and last a large box of nicely rolled bandages and soft cloths for the surgeons.

After remaining ten days with home folks and friends, I bid them farewell and started with my stores in quest of the boys. This was a slow and tedious job, and cost me much labor.

At Nashville I was detained a whole day. I reached Bowling Green in the night, and next morning found that the command had been sent off to some point, the provost marshal told me he would be able to inform me by 2 o'clock. I was ordered to Russellville. From Russellville to Clarksville.[2] Here I found my command had reached Hopkinsville the day before. I also found a wagon train loaded with ordnance and commissary stores almost ready to start for that place. I was lucky for once. I succeeded by hard work and main strength in getting my stores on this train. Then the provost marshal informed me he would have to put the train and about 800 convalescents in my charge to convey to Hopkinsville.

I was in hopes I would find some acquaintances, probably some of the Rifles, among the convalescents, but they were all Texans and Kentuckians, whose regiments had been attached to Gen. Alcorn's brigade.[3] When all was

33

ready, the provost marshal called me into his office and gave me instructions and orders:

"Try to make eight miles this evening, Lieutenant, so you can reach Hopkinsville tomorrow. Guard the train and stores, as an attempt may be made to capture or destroy them. Most of the convalescents have their arms and ammunition."

## Advent of the Measles

———◆——

I found a Lieutenant and a Sergeant among the convalescents. We soon formed them into line, or sort of a line; at least all who were in the vacant warehouse where they had been quartered. About one hundred men were out in the city hunting something to eat, or as we will soon see, to drink, and would join us as we marched through the town. An orderly was sent to pilot us out on the pike as far as Providence, a village some two miles from Clarksville, where I stopped the wagons and waited for my convalescents to close up. They straggled up slowly and to my dismay, I found them all drinking, and canteens filled with corn whiskey. I began to feel "in spots" and to study what I had best do. I began to feel the importance of this final duty assigned me, and how best proceed to guard these stores committed to my care. After going a mile or so I found running water, I placed my wagons in the best place I could select, I ordered my men into camp. I saw I could never reach the mill pond where I had been advised to camp, with this drinking crowd until long after night.

After resting an hour I sent my Lieutenant and Sergeant to detail a guard of twenty men. They soon returned and reported the whole turnout drunk, or drinking.

I said Lieutenant, go back and pick out twenty of the soberest men, take names, company and regiment, and assure them that if they did not report for guard duty at sunset, I would have the last one court martialed when we reached Hopkinsville. This brought them staggering in at sun down. I examined all the guns, and put five of the soberest men on guard. The others I made go into the tent and make themselves comfortable. In one hour I found them all sound asleep and succeeded in slipping all their canteens and hiding them. I kept the first relief on duty four hours to give the others time to sober up.

When the second relief was roused up every man asked the same question, "Where is my canteen."

My plan worked well, I had no trouble and no attack was made upon the train, but I passed a sleepless night and at sunrise started my train for Hopkinsville, which place I reached about sunset.

I found the officer I was to turn over the train to, ordered my convalescents to camp, and then hurried out to the fair grounds where my regiment was quartered, shook hands with the men and delivered their mail; the first they had received since leaving Iuka, ate a hearty supper, and was soon sleeping like a tired worn out soldier.

When Gen. Alcorn with his two regiments, the 1st and 3d Miss. reached Bowling Green he was given the 9th Tex. a very strong regiment and (I think) the 4th Ky. which made a very fine brigade of over 3000 muskets. The command was soon armed and equipped and he was ordered to proceed across the country to Hopkinsville.[1]

This was an exciting and instructing trip for the young soldiers. They marched through the country over one hundred miles, breaking up Union camps and capturing arms and other supplies which were greatly needed.

This was the first service of the young soldiers, and the night cold and frosty, consequently many contracted terrible colds, and many were taken really sick; and the great scourge of the Confederate army, measles, made its appearance in the brigade. This was something that astonished every one, even the surgeons. The common idea was that everybody had measles in early childhood, with a few exceptions, and would never have them again, but we found we had it down wrong, and when I reached my company, a very few days after the disease made its appearance I was astonished to learn that there were over one hundred cases in the brigade. We have all probably forgotten what a scourge this disease proved to our southern soldiers, and the readers of this story will be astonished when I tell them, that in the next three months the 9th Texas buried 96 men; the 3d Miss., 65 men; and the 1st Miss., 43, nearly all from measles or its sequel. More men than we lost in killed and wounded during the siege and open field fight at Fort Donelson. I was told that four of my company had measles, and that the sick were all in a large tobacco stemmery, which had been occupied as a general hospital for the present. After distributing the clothing I had brought, in company with Capt. Milam I visited the boys in the hospital, and what a sight greeted my eyes! About one hundred sick men in all stages of measles crowded in a room sixty by one hundred feet. The poor boys lying on the hard floor, with only one or two blankets under them, not even straw, and anything they could find for a pillow. Many sick and vomiting, many already showing unmistakable signs of blood poisoning.

"Is this the best Gen. Alcorn can do for his sick,

Captain? This wont do—our boys can't stay in this place, if anything better can be procured. They will all die, and we must get them out into private houses, if such a thing is possible, for I promised their parents, etc. at home I would see that they had the best attention possible if they should be taken sick. First, let us go and report conditions to Gen. Alcorn, I believe he will make a change, I don't believe he knows anything about it."

When we reported conditions to the General he rose from his seat, saying:

"I will go with you and visit my sick men, I have been so very busy since we reached the town I had overlooked them."

When we reached the barn and had gone through it from end to end he was very much shocked at the condition of the men and assured them they should have better quarters. As we walked back to camp the General asked if we had the medicine chest he had presented to the company before leaving home. I told him yes, that it had been of great service to the whole regiment while at Iuka, and that we had brought it with us.

"Take a file of men and go up town and find a vacant house, I am told the Union men all left when we came in, and where ever you find a vacant house that will answer the purpose, take possession and use every thing you find in and about the house, and make your sick comfortable, and attend to them yourself."

I thanked the General and asked permission to take the sick of Capt. Moseley's company² also, which was granted. Before night I had every one of my sick men on comfortable beds, between clean sheets. I also found a cooking stove and plenty of wood, but I must confess I did not relish taking possession of a man's residence and using every thing he had left in his kitchen, dining room and pantry, opening drawers and using blankets, sheets, towels, etc. It shocked my feelings very much, but then, I was learning to be a soldier, and this was a part of my military education—such is war! But circumstances justified the act. In less than two days every sick man in the brigade was in comparatively comfortable quarters. The epidemic rapidly increased and it taxed our ingenuity to provide beds for the new cases that were daily brought in from camp.[3]

# V

## *Sorrow, Death, Change*

———◆▶———

A great sorrow was soon to befall the Alcorn Rifles. Corporal Carter, one of the brightest boys in the company, was brought in from the camp ill with pneumonia. He had returned to camp a few days before, after a mild attack of measles, contrary to my orders. He felt well, and his great desire to see the boys and get back to his mess, caused him to slip off from the hopital and return to camp. This little act of indiscretion probably cost him his life, for his disease progressed rapidly to a fatal termination.

Rufus Byrd,[1] Orderly Sergeant for the Rifles, was a remarkable man in some respects. Forty years old, a man of great strength physically, well educated, raised a gentleman, a man of few words but of great firmness and decision of character, he probably had more influence over the boys than any other officer in the camp. But Rufe had his faults, and the greatest was a love of whisky. Sometimes this desire became ungovernable, and then the usually quiet, genial man became a tiger, and a very dangerous one.

For the first time since leaving home in July, this strange species of mania came over Rufus, and without leave or pass he slipped out of camp, went to town and found whisky. The result was a big fight with the police force. The tiger was captured of course, and lodged in the calaboose on a cold November evening.

That night we had a regular Kentucky blizzard, and the officers next morning found Rufus nearly frozen, and seemingly very ill. They warmed him up and made him comfortable, but he refused for several hours to give his name or tell where he belonged. Finally he asked to be taken to my hospital, and as the chief knew he was a soldier, sent him up immediately, expressing regrets at the occurrence.

When he arrived I was absent, having gone out to camp to see the boys, who told me of Byrd's absence from camp. I returned immediately as I knew where he would be found, and I felt satisfied he would need attention. Meeting Lieut. Howze,[2] who had gone to town in quest of Byrd, I was informed that he had been taken to the hospital, and that he seemed to be very ill, and anxious to see me. When I walked into his room, he raised up and said:

"I am very glad you have come. I was afraid I would lose my mind before you came, for I have a strange feeling in my head and lungs, and I believe I am going to die, and I want you to send me home for burial. I don't want to be buried up here in Kentucky. Will you do so?"

"I certainly will if such a thing is possible," I answered, "but I can't believe you are going to die. Is there anything else I can do for you?"

"Nothing," he answered. "You can now examine me and go to work, but your efforts will prove vain, for I feel certain I am going to die."

I examined the man carefully. He was very hoarse, sore throat, all the evidences of a severe catarrh, slight congestion of both lungs, but nothing sufficient to cause serious alarm; but his cool manner of talking of death and burial, the last subject I expected such a man to consider, staggered me, and I felt uneasy and afraid his case

41

was more serious than the symptoms indicated, so I called for Surgeon Hall,[3] and my old friend Dr. Raiford,[4] who, after a careful examination, laughed heartily at the patient's prognosis and the idea of his dying. Nevertheless he did die, and in a very short time, living only about thirty-six hours.

One hour later young Carter breathed his last. It was a sad day with the Rifles. The shock fell heavily upon them. These were the first to sicken and die, and the boys had not become hardened yet. Next morning the company marched in a body to the hospital to look for the last time upon the faces of their dead comrades.

It was a sad, sad scene. We dressed them in their new uniforms, put them in neat coffins, and in charge of Sergt. Yarbrough,[5] sent them home for burial. Letters I had written home in regard to Carter's illness failed to reach his father, and we can imagine the shock and the scare when the boy's dead body was driven up to his father's gate. Sergt. Yarbrough would not talk about it when he returned to camp but flatly told the boys he would never carry another one home for burial.

The poor old father succumbed to the blow, and ten days later he was buried beside his soldier boy. How often did such sad scenes occur in our Southland? The home folks had a harder time than we did, don't you forget it.

Just before Christmas I closed up my hospital and returned to camp. Measles had run its course, and the troops had become comparatively healthy, and there was no longer any use for the assistant hospitals. It was a little like getting back home again, and I enjoyed the change greatly.

Christmas in camp proved rather dull and uninteresting, still we had some fun getting up an extra dinner for the occasion, and the Rifles had turkey and to spare for the whole company, and in some mysterious way provided enough old-fashioned egg-nog to make everyone talk louder, feel better, and forget for a while at least, the old folks at home and the joys of Christmas festivities in the past.

About January 1st, 1862, Gen. Alcorn was superseded by Gen. Clark.[6] This change caused a great deal of dissatisfaction among men and officers. We had learned to love our general, who had been very kind and attentive to his men. In his farewell address he stated that the order from the war department was unexpected and cruel, that he had expended ten thousand dollars of his own money in equipping his brigade, and preparing it for service, and now when it was ready for service, ready for the field, to be forced to give it up and the proud privilege of leading it into battle, caused him deep sorrow.

Changes were now taking place rapidly, and the campaign was opening in earnest. Various rumors were in the air—something is going to happen.

# VI

## *Tragedy at Fort Donelson*

———————◆▶———————

The latter part of January (I don't remember dates) orders were sent out to strike tents, cook 3 days rations and be ready to move at a moment's warning. This meant work, work, work. Everything must be packed, loaded on the wagon train and sent back—where? The troops marched to Clarksville and then boats to Dover, a small village on the Cumberland river, about one mile above Fort Donelson.[1] This village of one hundred or more inhabitants was incircled by the breastworks we erected, commencing at the Fort, and sweeping round in a semi-circle to, or near, the river a mile above the village. This is a rough sketch of the earthworks we were sent down to build, and then defend against the advancing host of Gen. Grant, whose guns were already thundering against Fort Henry on the Tennessee river some twelve or fifteen miles away.[2]

Fortunately we had time to prepare for the storm that would soon burst upon us, and the men worked with a will. Our military education was now rapidly progressing and we were preparing for final examination or commencement. A good deal of time was required to reduce Fort Henry, time to transfer the fleet from the Tennessee to the Cumberland. Time for Gen. Grant to move his army across the country from Fort Henry to our breastworks around Donelson.

Forrest's cavalry contested every inch of ground between the rivers, and it was here the cavalier won his spurs and manifested those fine fighting qualities which afterwards made him a terror to his enemies, and the idol of the southern army of the Confederacy.

The Federal fleet announced their arrival by opening fire upon the Fort late one evening,[3] and kept up a brisk fire for some time, and we had the thrilling pleasure of listening to the roar of heavy artillery, which made the earth tremble where we stood.

The next day a combined attack was made upon the Fort and breastworks without result. This continued daily for nearly a week; the Federals steadily moving to the right (our left) and gradually encircling us with batteries and armed men. A child could see how the drama would end. The sixth night, if I remember correctly, a rumor was current that an attempt would be made next morning to drive the enemy back; if successful, the garrison would march up the river and make their escape. This report proved partly true. At daylight (Saturday morning) our brigade, with other troops, marched out, and formed in line at right angles to our works, and were ordered to move forward through the dense woods until they "find the enemy, then charge, rout him, re-form line and move forward again." I don't know that these were the orders but that is the way the battle was fought. This feat of charging and routing the enemy was successfully accomplished four or five times, and by 2 p.m. the enemy was driven back two miles or more, and the movement ended. Why was it? There we stood awaiting orders, expecting every moment to hear the order: "By the left flank march." But no order came, no effort made to get out of the trap. Why was it? I have never read an explanation of this strange thing. The escape of the whole garrison may have been an impossibility, but that assaulting column, of several thousand men, could have walked away at their leisure, with Forrest for a rear guard.[4]

By 5 p.m. we were all back where we started—in the ditches, wonder stricken, dazed. I have no language to describe our feelings. The loss to the brigade was trifling owing to the densely wooded country through which we fought, but chiefly owing, I think, to bad shooting.

At 2 p.m. that Saturday night we were marched out into an old field and formed into line, and we now felt certain we were going. It was a dark night, but as the ground was covered with snow, light enough to march. We waited impatiently for orders to move forward and make our escape. Waited, marking time to keep our poor feet from freezing, until daylight, and then were ordered to march back, and stack arms in rear of our works. Just then a line of cavalry was seen moving out on the left of our works going up the river, and we thought we were going to fight again, but it was the bold Forrest, riding out of the trap.[5]

Then the truth began to dawn upon us, that we had been sacrificed, surrendered to the foe. As it grew lighter an officer rode up and unfurled a white flag to place upon our breastworks. The men refused to let him put it up. He rode further up the line and made a second attempt, with similar results, when he rode on out of sight with his white rag flying.

It is impossible to describe what I witnessed in the next hour. Many seemed stunned, and had nothing to say. Many were wringing their hands and weeping hysterically. Officers were breaking their swords and throwing them away.

The Federal cavalry rode slowly down our breastworks to the extreme left, halted and faced toward the prisoners. The infantry marched upon our rear, formed a line facing toward us. The sight of the triumphant enemy marching in to take possession produced a strange effect upon our men. Eyes were dried, emotion vanished, and an unconquerable set of men awaited the orders of their captains. Walking up to Lieut. Howze, of the Rifles, I said:

"Good-bye, Will."

"Where are you going?"

"I'm going to make my escape."

"Are you crazy?"

"No. Good-bye."

"Have you wings?"

"Good-bye."

And shaking hands with every member of the company, I walked rapidly toward the Federal lines closing up in our rear.

# VII

## *The Escape*

———◆——

Had I been a private I would have slipped off at early
dawn when we were ordered to march back and stack
arms. I think I would have had little difficulty in making
my escape then. Many did succeed, as you shall see further
on. Some escaped with Forrest's cavalry, riding out behind
the troopers. But I could not feel certain that we would
be surrendered, and I could see no necessity for it that
Sabbath morning.

It was reported that little or no impression had been
made upon the Fort by the fleet. Our men had repulsed
every attack upon our breastworks, and we had meat and
bread night and morning. Why should we surrender just
then? Had I left my command early in the morning and
the surrender had taken place later on, it would have
looked like desertion. But when the arms were stacked,
the Federal cavalry in position in front and their infantry
rapidly closing up in the rear, I could make no mistake.
The time had come for me to speak, or forever hold my
peace.

When I reached the Federal lines to my astonishment
they stepped aside and permitted me to pass without a
word, and I walked rapidly down the path towards Dover.
Good luck so far, thought I, as I walked across the hills
and gullies toward the little town. What next? What shall
I do now? My mind was running at a rapid speed, but I
could only move forward. Suddenly a thought struck me.

I must get rid of my sword. Instantly I unbuckled my good blade, the pride of all young officers, and let it slide into a gully as I walked over the plankway. As I drew near the first house on the outskirts of the village, I noticed an old man standing at the yard gate, looking over the hills at the sad drama taking place at the breastworks. As I approached I thought the old man looked peculiarly sad, as he gazed upon the scene, and the main idea that I had stumbled upon a southern friend, caused my heart to quicken its beat. Drowning men catch at straws. Turning up to the gate and speaking to the old man, I said:

"You see I am a southern soldier, and you know I am a prisoner. Now, the thought of lying in prison for months, probably years, is perfectly horrible, far worse than death upon the battlefield. I have determined to make my escape, if I lose my life in the attempt. Will you help me?"

"Captain," said the old man in astonishment, "how do you expect to get out of this place? The river yonder is at flood tide, and Grant's army is all around you, and how can an old man help you?"

"Well, my friend," I answered, encouraged by the old man's kindly look. "If you can only hide me and procure me some old clothes, so I can get out of my uniform, I will manage the rest."

"But if the Yankees should find you hidden in my house, don't you suppose they would burn it? And this poor house is all we have left, and my only son, my only help, is in the southern army."

"I don't think they will do that (grabbing at straws) and if they find me, I will make a clean breast of it, and take all the consequences."

"Well," said the old man slowly, as if he was calcu-

lating the chances, "go yonder and talk to the old woman;
if she'll hide you, I will try and find you some old
clothes."

I stepped quickly across the yard to the old woman's
side, for I felt confident I could touch a wife and mother's
heart.

"Madam, you see I am a southern soldier, and you
know that the fortunes of war have made me a prisoner,
and unless I can make my escape from this place, I am
doomed to lie in some loathsome northern prison for
months, and probably for years. I have a wife and child
at home, and the thought of wearing my life out in prison
and never seeing them again, is worse than death, and
more than I can bear. Won't you hide me until your husband can procure me other clothing? If I can get out of
this uniform I feel confident I can make my escape."

The old lady's eyes began filling with tears, and by
the time I had finished my little speech, her mind was fully
made up. She never thought of danger to herself or
property.

"Follow me," she said, "and keep silent. There are
two Federal soldiers in the front room nursing two
wounded men."

I walked in where the wounded men were lying. The
nurses seemed surprised at seeing a Confederate officer,
but I spoke to them politely, and asked after the wounded
men, and finding one of them suffering intensely, I told the
man to get cold water and bathe the wounded hand, and
try and get him a dose of morphine. I told them I was a
surgeon, but had no medicine. The men seemed more
surprised, and asked me to have a seat, but I told them I
had no time to talk, and walked on closing the door

behind me, passing through the next room which was a closed hall, into the third room, where I found the old lady waiting for me.

"Wasn't you afraid to stop and talk to those soldiers."

"Oh no, I wanted to make friends. I would like to make friends with the whole Yankee army this morning, but really I wanted to impress them that I was a surgeon, and if I am recaptured, I shall claim to be a surgeon, for my chances to get south will be greater. Please remember this."

The old lady reached under a bed and drawing out a light ladder, placed it to a trap door in the floor above and bade me ascend to my new quarters and make myself as comfortable as possible. When I reached the room and had replaced the trap door, I looked around, and to my astonishment found myself in a perfectly bare room, no chairs, bed, or anything else. "A bare chance," thought I, but I was under cover, hid, and was thankful.

# VIII

## Days of Anxiety

———◆———

Seating myself on the floor I called a halt to hold a council of war. What shall I do? What can I do? How long can I stand this? After my brisk walk I was already growing cold, and possibly mine hostess in her excitement won't think of me for hours. Nothing better suggesting, I removed my boots and determined to inspect my quarters and see what I could find.

Crawling over the log walls, for no doors had been sawed out, I reached the room in the further end of the building, over the room occupied by the Federal soldiers, and to my delight found with other plunder packed away, two large feather beds. These I removed one at a time to my end of the room, and placing them on the floor, I crawled between them, and soon becoming warm, fell asleep.

How long I slept I could not tell, but I was aroused by martial music, and men marching near the house, and creeping to a crack in the weatherboarding, I looked out and found it was nearly night. It was light enough for me to discover that my dear comrades, the brave defenders of Fort Donelson were marching by to the river, to be transported to their northern prison. Their shouts and jesting showed the unconquerable spirit of the men. The sight chilled my blood, but I stood for some time peering through the twilight, to catch if possible, a glimpse of some familiar face, until the chattering of my teeth warned me to seek again my virtuous couch.

It would be difficult to imagine the thoughts that passed rapidly through my brain as I lay there shivering between those feather beds, and could now calmly and coolly take in the whole situation. But my thoughts were chiefly of my brave comrades who were being hurried through the rain and snow to the river, to be crowded on transports and conveyed to prison.

Poor fellows! Wet, cold, hungry and worn out by a hard week of fighting and watching in the muddy, freezing ditches around Dover. How can frail humanity stand such hardships and exposure?

But I had only a faint conception of the horrors of that voyage from Dover to Alton and Johnson's Island, until eighteen months later around the camp-fires in Mississippi, I heard it from the survivors who were permitted by a kind Providence to return to Dixie.[1]

Other thoughts also crowded through my brain, as tired and hungry I lay in that dark garret and could only think. Thoughts of home, its comforts and joys; thoughts of the young wife and little boy waiting there; thoughts of the gray-haired sire who patiently waited to hear the result of the siege; thoughts of the dear sisters who were ever praying for me, and believed me dead or a prisoner. But there is an end to all things, so there was an end to those pleasant and horrible thoughts, for tired nature's sweet restorer came to the relief of the lonely soldier.

After a good long nap I was awakened by a tap at the little door. Crawling out from beneath my feather bed, I raised my door, when the dear old woman whispered:

"I thought I'd never wake you. I have been knocking

here for some time. You must be very tired. Take up the candle and I will hand up your supper, for I know you must be hungry, I had to wait until the soldiers went to sleep."

The mere thought of supper, aside from the sweet odor that ascended through that trap door, would have made my mouth water. The reader must know that the garrison had been constantly in the ditches for a week or more, and a good square meal had not been eaten in that time. The cooking had been done by detail down on the river, a fourth of a mile from the men, and brought in and handed the men as they sat behind the breastworks, just at dark, and about daylight in the morning, so if a soldier got a good sized piece of bread and meat twice a day, and a pint of coffee at night, he was fortunate and satisfied. I had eaten nothing for about thirty hours. Up came the supper, fried ham and eggs, good lye hominy, biscuits, butter and coffee.

Reader, did you ever feel your stomach dance a jig? Did you ever return heartfelt thanks to God for your bread? I ate slowly, as slow as I could, and tried to chew my food thoroughly, for I had serious thoughts, or fears of making myself sick, and the idea of getting sick under such circumstances was not at all pleasant. When the dishes were handed down they hardly needed washing. "What time is it, mother?" as I passed down the light. "Nearly one o'clock." "Good night." Down went the trap door, and into bed I slipped to keep warm and think, for no man could sleep with that supper on his stomach, not even a soldier.

The hours passed slowly away, and it seemed an age from that supper time until the Federal drums aroused

Grant's sleeping host. As it grew light I crawled out of my warm bed to peep out and get an idea of the weather. Going to my little crevice in the wall, I discovered that it was a drizzly, foggy morning, and I soon ascertained that it was still disagreeably cold. I am afraid this part of my story will prove uninteresting to most of my readers. I can't help that, I know that it was horribly uninteresting to the writer.

Well, I thought, there is nothing to be done but lie in bed, keep comfortable and await developments. Monday passed slowly away. Voices could be heard below, but although I pressed my ear to the floor, I could hear but little. I heard the family, or rather the old folks and the soldiers sit down to breakfast. I heard the rattling of cups and plates, heard them get up and disperse, but not a word of the conversation while eating. I wonder if the good woman will hand up my breakfast this morning? Not that I cared to eat or was hungry, but I desired to see a human face and to ask questions. I found that curiosity was very much sharpened by solitary confinement.

I could not help thinking of and wishing for that suit of old clothes promised me. How precious old clothes became, and how hateful the fine suit of Confederate gray I wore. The suit had been sent me from home by a very dear friend, Dr. W. M. Compton,[2] and had been trimmed by some precious Southern girls at Hopkinsville, Ky., where I had been quartered during the winter, and was prized above money, but now I would willingly exchange it for the meanest, dirtiest suit of one of the ebony camp followers of Grant's army.

The day wore away at last, and darkness enveloped the earth again. Supper passed off below, and the hum of voices satisfied me that there were many others besides the family present, and I rightly conjectured they were Federal soldiers.

At last the tap at my little door warned me that my supper had come, and raising the door the dear old face appeared, and she whispered:

"Ain't you most starved? I couldn't help it, I had to arrange to cook for the officers of an Artillery company camped close by, so as to get food. Some of them have been in the house all day, and I was afraid you would cough or make a noise and betray yourself."

"Mother," I said, "I have suffered very little from cold or hunger, but when will you get that suit of old clothes so I can come down from this room, and watch for a chance to escape?"

"A neighbor promised to bring them tonight, but from some cause he has failed, and it is too late now, as it is 11 o'clock. You must not worry."

"I am not worrying, my friend, don't think that, but I am growing miserably impatient to get on terra firma again, and make some effort to escape from this place."

"I have brought you something to eat. Tomorrow I will not be able to get you but one meal a day."

"Do you know whether the army is on the move, or not?"

"No I do not. The old man is trying to learn all he can for you."

"Have all the prisoners been sent off?"

"I think so. I learned that from the officers. But I must go now."

She passed up a plate filled with biscuits, cake and boiled ham, then taking down the dishes returned for the light, and again left the prisoner in darkness.

## IX

# From Captain to Cook

---◆---

Tuesday and Tuesday night passed slowly away making no change in my surroundings. I only grew more impatient and restless as the hours dragged wearily along. On Wednesday night I not only received my good supper but also the coveted old clothes. My heart throbbed with thankfulness at the mere thought of getting down from that garret. I could hardly content myself to eat my supper before dressing up in my new suit, and as that suit of "old clothes" enabled me to make my escape, I think it is entitled to a full description, if it is possible for me to describe them. The pants were of a dark gray cloth usually known as "salt and pepper" but had been worn until the pepper was hardly discernable. They had been worn by some one whose weight must have approached 200 pounds and as I was a small man weighing 140 I could hardly hope for a fit, and when I drew them on I was astonished at the length of the former owner.

By shortening suspenders and using my pocket knife at the other end a very respectable fit was at last effected. I found them very roomy for cold weather, and well ventilated besides. The vest was yellow, a dingy yellow, resembling the cloth that comes around a canvassed ham. The coat was originally of checked goods, but the checks were hardly discernable, from long service. The lining was delapidated, and the sleeves had air-holes at the elbow.

The owner was doubtless a small man for in it I found a tight fit. The cap was a daisy. It was made of the tanned skin of the American coon with the "narative" left in its proper place, and was a perfect fit.

When I descended the ladder the old couple began to laugh, and laughed until I feared their sides would split.

"Captain," said the old man, "I saw you before you went up that ladder in your handsome gray uniform, and the change is so great I am bound to laugh. I think you are perfectly disguised. I don't think your own men would know you if they were to meet you on the street tomorrow."

I was perfectly satisfied with my new suit and believed it would prove a success and seating myself began to quiz the old man in regard to the situation of the Federal army. He thought little or no advance had been made. That the General was waiting for the return of his transport which had carried the prisoners off, to convey his troops up the Cumberland. That the bulk of the army was in and around Dover, between the Tennessee and Cumberland rivers.[1]

Then I must go north into Kentucky and make a wide circuit around Clarksville to reach Nashville. So we must look around tomorrow and find some way for me to cross the river.

"I am afraid that will be a difficult job," said the old man, "for the boats are tied up on this side of the river, and their crews are in camp on the other side, and the road runs right through their camp."

"Are the country people coming into town yet?" I asked.

"I do not know. I have not seen any one from the country. I understand there is no going out, but as you now have your disguise I will look out for a chance to put you across the river."

"Well I will come down in the morning and probably I can help you find a chance. Please let me have your shaving apparatus to take off the little beard I have, as I wish to look as young and boyish as possible, and I will play general waiting boy for you and your wife and if the Federal officers ask who I am, just say that I am a country boy who came over the river before the surrender, and has not been able to get back, and that you are feeding him until the way is open for him to return home."

After a careful shave I returned to my quarters in the loft, full of hope but rather gloomy at the prospect of making an early escape from my perilous situation. In the morning I was up by the time the old couple were dressed, and descended to the kitchen to commence my duties, and soon began in a small way to pay the debt of gratitude I owed the dear old people, by making myself generally useful. When the Federal officers came in to breakfast they seemed a little surprised, I thought, at seeing a new cook turning the batter cakes and pouring out the coffee.

"Well," said one of them, "where did you strike your new cook?"

My heart jumped suddenly into my throat, and I fairly held my breath, until the old man quietly answered as requested the night before.

"Tom," said the old man, "you had better put a little wood on the fire."

And Tom was glad to reach the open air for the perspiration was becoming troublesome, and he felt a sensation of faintness pass over his frame.

The cool morning air soon restored him, and he felt that the Rubicon was passed and he would have no more trouble from those officers. The day passed away quietly and without incident. Tom's eyes were everywhere and his ears open to every sound. After the officers returned to their quarters that night the old man said he had learned, just before leaving town, that several citizens had crossed over the river to see Gen. Grant, and to take the oath.

"Now if my information is correct, you may get across the river sooner than you expect. Now don't permit this information to raise your hopes too high, for the report may be false, and if it is true, you may fail or something prevent your getting off with the first who recross. I will try and see the ferryman in the morning and make the necessary arrangements. The ferryman is a good southern man, and can be depended on, so I advise you to go to bed and get a good night's rest, for we don't know what is before us in this world."

After using the old man's razor again, thoroughly and carefully, I ascended the ladder again, and I hoped for the last time to lie down and plan different ways of escape, but to sleep very little.

## X

## *Eluding the Federals*

————◄•►————

The next morning after an early breakfast the old man started up town, and I anxiously watched him as he walked across the hollow, up the hill beyond, and across the guard lines into the little village. I watched him closely because I thought I would have to travel the same road when I started. Hope and fear alternately held possession of my heart, and the hours passed slowly away. About 10 o'clock I discovered the old man passing the guard lines and slowly walking homeward. I was waiting at the woodpile for him.

"Did you see me pass the guard lines, yonder?"

"Yes," I said.

"You will have to go just as you saw me come. If you succeed in passing the guard lines keep straight forward through the village until you reach the river then down the bank until you find the ferryboat. When the ferryman and citizens arrive, go on with them and obey the boatman's orders. He will know you by your cap. You must start, for you have no time to lose." I heard and drank in these directions with joy unspeakable, and going into the house, hurriedly expressed my thanks for their kindness. I gave the old lady the last ten dollar State bill[1] I had— part of the funds I started from home with—as a small testimonial of my gratitude, bade them farewell and started down the path toward Dover whistling and throwing rocks at the snowbirds along the way, determined to play the green backwoods country boy that my garb indicated. As I drew near the first line the thought occurred to me to pass midway between them and thus avoid close inspection, approaching the lines I was promptly halted by the sentry on the left. Paying no attention to the command which I distinctly heard, I sauntered on whistling and looking toward the sentry on my right, until I had crossed the line, when a more emphatic "halt," in a loud tone, warned me that I had better heed. Turning carelessly toward the sentry whose gun was leveled at me, I said:

"Did you speak to me, Mister?"

"Yes, can't you hear? Where in the h—l are you going?"

"I'm jest gwine up town."

"Do you live here?"

"In course I does, I lives over thar in that house, and I am jest gwine up town."

"Then go on, you d—— fool," said the pious soldier, as he lowered his musket, and the "d—— fool" went ahead, whistling, feeling an inch taller in his boots, and thankful for small favors and compliments. As I approached the second line of sentries, which I could plainly see from the house, I discovered that this was a special guard around a park of Artillery. They permitted me to pass unchallenged, thinking probably it was useless to challenge such a boy. I walked through this immense park of Artillery, looking at the guns and now and then asking some foolish boyish question, which caused more than once a hearty laugh among the soldiers. Following directions I soon reached the river, and had a sight, for the first time, of the dreaded gunboats.[2] A number of which were tied up along the river bank. I did not stop to admire or investigate the monsters for fear I would be too late for the ferryboat. Keeping down the river I soon found the boat, and sitting down, waited for the citizens. Pretty soon I saw a number coming in my direction on another street, but they turned and came toward the boat. When they arrived and walked on the boat, I walked up to the post. The ferryman called for their passes and then looking straight at me said:

"Turn her loose."

I quietly unhooked and unwound the chain and threw it aboard with all the grace of an experienced boatman.

"Shove her off," was the next order, and grasping the pole used for the purpose, I shoved that craft from shore—just then I felt strong enough to push off the Great Eastern[3] or Noah's Ark. A prayer of thankfulness went up from my heart, as I bade a silent farewell to Fort Donelson. But I had no time for pious or sentimental reflections, as the ferryman ordered me to seize the oar and pull for dear life. The current was dangerously swift, and carried the boat a long way down stream, before we began to pull upon the other side. At last we reached the shore and springing out upon the bank I pulled up the boat and wrapped the chain around the sapling and helped the dear old Union brothers to land.

The passengers paid their fares and put off in a body down the river.

"My friend," said I, looking at the boiling, surging river, "weren't you afraid to cross that stream?"

"Well," he said, "it was a little dangerous, but I saw I had an experienced hand at the oar, and I wasn't much afraid."

He said this with a peculiar smile. I handed him a two dollar bill, the last money I had.

"I thank you for bringing me over that terrible river and will never forget the kindness. Now show me the Clarksville road and give me directions, for I must go."

"Keep right up the river. Some distance above the road turns to the left, then keep the plainest road."

I shook his horny hand and started up the river walking rapidly. The road led right through the camp of boatmen, but they neither noticed or challenged me. A mile above the road turned to the left up a long hill and I soon found myself in a densely wooded country. At the top of the hill I met a man on a mule riding in a gallop towards town.

"Hello, friend, are there any Yankees camped on this road?"

"There is a brigade of Federal soldiers camped a mile or so above, but I don't know that they are Yankees."

I knew at once that I had struck a Union man.

"They are the troops I am looking for, I knew they were somewhere up this road. I am much obliged to you."

He spoke to his mule and passed on.

As soon as the fellow passed out of sight, I sprang out of the road on the left into the bushes and started directly across the hills and hollows at right angles to the road I had left. My object was to flank that Federal brigade, and as I was a stranger in the county, knew nothing of the direction of the road, had no compass, not even the sun to guide me, for it was cloudy, I determined to travel in this direction a couple of miles, and then turn square to the right. I would then be on a parallel line with the Clarksville road and out of danger from those Federals.[4]

THE AUTHOR
Dr. LeGrand J. Wilson

THE HIGH-WATER MARK OF THE CONFEDERA

LITTLE TOWN OF GETTYSBURG, PENNSYLVANIA

JAMES L. ALCORN

JEFFERSON DAVIS

JEFFERSON

JEREMIAH SANDERS GAGE

JOSEPH R. DAVIS

ES ON PARADE

PROVOST-MARSHAL'S OFFICE

CONFEDERATE CAMP NEAR CORINTH

R. W. LOCKE

THE LOCKE HOME

## *A Soldier Befriended*

———◆———

I soon found that I was crossing a very rough section of country. High hills and deep hollows, and covered with a dense undergrowth of bushes, which was in my favor. In about a mile it grew more open, and getting upon the top of a high ridge, I stopped, and looking around in every direction, could discover no settlement or farm house, and I naturally concluded that I was traveling through a very thinly settled country. On I went down hill at double quick, up hill not so fast.

The snow was soft and melting, hence I made little noise walking through the bushes. As I reached the top of one of the ridges I was crossing, I was considerably startled at seeing right ahead of me down the side of the ridge, a Yankee soldier, his hands in his pockets, in the attitude of listening, his gun leaning against his shoulder and his back toward me. I was too tired to run and if I run he will shoot me before I can get out of sight. There is but one course to pursue. I had the down grade, and crossing that intervening space of forty or fifty feet in a twinkling, and as the Yankee turned to see what was coming behind him, I dropped by his side, grasped his gun and ordered him to surrender. The boy, for he was a great big boy with a Yankee overcoat on, stood trembling before me.

"What are you doing here?" I asked.

"I am trying to kill a deer, sir. Mother is out of meat

and we have two sick soldiers at our house and she sent me out to try and kill a deer. Don't you hear my dogs? They are trailing one now." The boy was trembling with fright.

"Did you say there were sick soldiers at your house?"

"Yes sir."

"Are they Yankees or Rebels?"

The boy hesitated.

"Speak out. You need not be afraid."

"They are Rebels," he answered.

"I am glad to hear that. I am a Southern soldier and I crossed the river and made my escape this morning."

"Lord, Mister, I thought you were a Yankee, and you like to have scared me to death."

"Well, you need not be frightened any longer. Are you acquainted with the country?"

"Yes, sir."

"Can you pilot me around the Yankees on the Clarksville road, and put me on the road above them?"

"Yes, sir."

"Then shoulder your gun, strike out and I will follow you."

"Mister," said the boy, "please go down to the house with me, so mother will know where I am, and not be uneasy."

"All right, go ahead."

When we reached the house I found the sick soldiers as the boy had said. I also found a very intelligent woman in his mother. When I told her what I wished, she said quickly:

"I don't think you can make your escape that way;

the country is full of bushwhackers, and the meanest Union men in Southwest Kentucky.[1] I can put you on a road that you will have no difficulty in finding, and you will find good southern friends all along to help you."

I thanked the good woman, but felt more thankful to the kind Providence that had directed me to her door. She then gave me directions to Dr. White's, sixteen miles distant, a dinner of milk, bread and butter, and sent her son some distance with me to put me on the right way. I started on my walk with a light heart and a full commissary department. Just before dark I toiled up a long, steep hill into the Kentucky barrens, and saw before me the desired haven of rest, the handsome residence of Dr. White.[2] I called at the gate, and an old negro woman answered.

"Is Dr. White at home?"

"No sah. He started south yesterday with all the colored folks and the stock, to try to save them from the Yankees."

"I was directed to come here and spend the night, and do not think I can go any further. Can I stay all night with you?"

"Is you a 'Federate soldier, Massa?"

"Yes," I answered.

"Den come right in. Massa lef' me here to take keer of the place, an' tole me to take keer of any 'Federate soldiers what might come along. Jes come right in."

I walked in, and when I reached the portico the old negress exclaimed:

"Lord, Massa, you is dressed mighty funny for a soldier."

67

"Yes," I answered, "this old suit of clothes helped me to make my escape from the Yankees, and they are very much prized just now."

"Jes walk right into de parlor, Massa. Dere is another soldier in there."

On reaching the parlor I was very much surprised and delighted to find my old regimental commissary, Capt. Gannaway,[3] who made his escape early Sunday morning, crossing the river before the surrender. Old Aunty soon had us a good supper, and we were ready for bed as soon as we related our adventures. But my feet were so completely done up with my long walk, that I found it difficult to sleep. I bathed and greased them, and wrapped them in soft cloths, but they throbbed and burned so terribly, it was late before tired nature asserted her rights.

The next morning my feet were so swollen and tender I found it almost impossible to get on my boots after splitting them up in front, and I was afraid I would not be able to walk at all. This was discouraging. Both knew that it was important to go ahead, that a rapid advance would be made by the Federals, so after an early breakfast we started for a farm house a half mile away, hoping to be able to get some conveyance, Gannaway helping me along as best he could. Fortunately we found a good southern man to help us—ready and willing to help us.

Capt. G. bought a good horse, saddle and bridle from him, and the old man putting his only saddle on another horse assisted me to mount and springing upon a third horse with a blanket for a saddle, told us to follow. I remonstrated, desiring to ride the bareback horse myself, but he would not hear to it, so away we went, over hill and dale, through woods and fields, our guide paying no attention to roads or paths, except to avoid them. After riding some sixteen miles at this breakneck speed, the old man rode up to a newly settled place, and springing off his horse as he rode up, he said:

"Get down gentlemen. My son-in-law lives here. We will get our dinner, and I will get him to take you to Judge Overton's,[4] sixteen miles further on. You will find the Judge an old time southern gentleman, and he will help you on tomorrow."

After dinner the young man brought out two fresh horses. Expressing our thanks, we shook hands with our friend in need, and started on another John Gilpin ride of sixteen miles. Judge Overton seemed really glad to see us, glad to help us, as all these good southern people were. The poor widow back yonder under the hill nursing the two sick soldiers, and who sent me on this way, knew them as patriots and she had the same royal blood in her own veins, and would do all she could for the southern soldier.

Judge Overton treated us with the greatest kindness, special attention being given to my bruised and swollen feet. The old gentleman was greatly amused at my disguise, and had me tell him over and over of my escape. We found here six more soldiers, Kentuckians, who made their escape, and crossed the river early Sunday morning of the surrender.

# XII

## A Sore-Footed Rebel

———◄•►———

After a good night's rest I found my feet much improved, and that I could walk if it was necessary. Judge Overton sent us out to the pike in two miles of Clarksville,[1] but was afraid to risk his wagon and team in Clarksville as the enemy might have reached the town during the night. Capt. Gannaway said he would ride ahead and reconnoiter and if he found the way clear, would go into town and learn all he could in regard to the military situation, and the best route for us to travel to reach the Confederate lines.

When we reached the pike we separated, the Kentuckians going north. Alone I started on my way. As I was nearing Providence, a landing where we had taken the boat on our way to Donelson two or three weeks before, a band struck up a lively air down at the landing. Walking to the top of the hill and looking over, I found a transport disgorging troops, and a regiment forming on the bank. I looked but a moment, and facing about I took the back track, and started up the pike at a lively pace for a sore footed Rebel. It was astonishing the beneficial effect the sight of those Yankees had upon my sore feet.

It began to rain a cold drizzling rain, that penetrated my old clothes, and was decidedly uncomfortable. Nearing a fine residence I determined to stop out of the rain and make some inquiries. I had been thinking, and I remembered that a southern man lived on or near this road, by the name of Clardy. While I was in charge of the hospital at Hopkinsville during the winter, this man brought chickens, butter, eggs, and other good things to our sick, and he did this more than once. I knew that he was made of the right stuff, and now if I can find him I will find another friend in need. Walking up to the door I knocked; an elderly lady answered the call, and when she opened the door and flashed her eyes over her visitor, she hesitated, drew back, and seemed about to close the door. I said:

"I called, Madam, to get out of this cold rain, and to inquire for a friend who lives near you."

"Walk in to the fire and have a chair. Who is your friend you wish to meet?"

"William Clardy."

"Col. Clardy is one of our neighbors and lives a mile north. You will have no trouble to find his residence."

"I am glad to hear that. Do you suppose I will find him at home?"

"Yes, this is his birthday, and a good many friends dine with him today. My husband started to his house just before you called."

"Perhaps I will help him eat that dinner."

"Will you allow me to ask where you are from sir?"

"I am from Fort Donelson, Madam."

"Are you a Confederate soldier?"

"I am, Madam. 1st Lieutenant Company F. 1st Mississippi regiment. Thanks to this disguise that astonished you so much when you opened your door, I made my escape three days ago, and I am trying to get back within our lines. But I must be going as the rain has ceased and

71

I am anxious to get to that birthday dinner."

"Wait a few moments," said the lady, as she left the room. In a short time she returned, and put around my shoulders a heavy, warm, black Talma or cloak, then wrapping a beautiful yellow nubia around my ears and head, she said feelingly:

"I hope, now, you will be more comfortable, and that you will get home safely."

"God bless you," I said, as I grasped that southern mother's hand, and pressing it to my lips, I stepped out upon the highway, and resumed my walk. I soon reached Col. Clardy's, and as I walked up to the yard gate, several gentlemen came out upon the portico, and attracted by my cap, stood looking at me, as I supposed. Before I reached the steps, Clardy recognized me and exclaimed:

"Good Lord, Lieutenant, I thought you were at Donelson!"

"I was until day before yesterday, when I made my escape from the bluecoats."

"How did you get away?"

"Wait a moment and I believe I can show you." I took off my nubia and laid it aside, then my cloak, and stepping out, I said:

"In this handsome disguise I simply walked out of the Federal army, the easiest job I ever undertook."

"Where did you get those clothes? But stop. I see you are wet. Get there by the fire, and I will see if I can't make you more comfortable."

Pretty soon I was called into another room, where I found water, soap, towels, and a chair covered with dry clothing.

"Lieutenant, I think my clothes will fit you better than

72

those you have on, and I want to make an exchange with you. That cap I shall prize above money, and keep it as a souvenir of this horrid war, so bathe, dress up, and come out to dinner, for I am dying to hear your story."

In a short while I was ready for dinner, and much improved in feelings and appearance. While eating a first-class birthday dinner, enthused by the presence of twelve or fifteen loyal, bighearted ladies and gentlemen, I gave a graphic, and probably the most brilliant description of the siege, the surrender and my escape that I have been able to write or think. The inspiration of the moment turned my young tongue loose, and if I put on too much coloring, no one will ever be able to find it out. After a smoke with the gentlemen, I said to them:

"I want your best advice and directions as to the route I shall take to get back into our lines, for I must be traveling."

"Not until morning, Lieutenant. You must remain with us tonight."

"No, Colonel, I must push forward. The Yanks are getting too close to me."

"Where are any Yanks?"

"At Providence, in Clarksville, and probably in a mile of us now. I saw them landing at Providence, and I knew I would have to flank Clarksville, so faced about and came in this direction, and you really owe this visit of mine to the Yanks."

"Lieutenant, I have a fine horse left with me by Col. Sugg, of the ——th Tennessee regiment, who told me to give him to some Confederate soldier if the Yankees got into this country, and it seems that they have surprised us and I expect we will lose all our stock. If you will risk it

73

and remain all night, I will send down to my farm and get him for you."

"Colonel, I can't afford to run any risks. I wouldn't be recaptured for forty horses. I must push right ahead."

"Well," he said, "I will do the best I can for you." He had a mule brought out. "That is the only thing I have for you to ride."

"Colonel, how shall I ever repay you for all this kindness."

"Just get back to the army and make a faithful soldier to the end."

"I will do it," I said.

The Colonel and one of his guests rode with me to pilot me across a creek, and gave me directions to a place to spend the night. Just as we rode out of the lawn upon the highway, up came Capt. Gannaway in a gallop, and rode right up to us, failing to recognize me on account of my change of apparel.

"Hello, Captain, where are you going?"

He knew my voice, and looking at me in astonishment said: "Where have you been?"

"Let me ask you the same question. You left me this morning without leave, saying you were going to hunt the enemy. Several hours later you come dashing up to the column and demand explanations."

"Well," he said laughing, "I have had a terrible race. After leaving you this morning I rode on into Clarksville without seeing any sight of the enemy. When I reached the center of town I rode right on a regiment of Cavalry. I saw them first, and turning my horse into a side street, I soon had him at full speed. They were after me in a moment and chased me five or six miles, but my horse was best, and they finally gave up the chase and went back."

"A pretty good report, Captain, and now I will answer your question. I have been among my friends. I have had a good day, a most pleasant, happy day, and now I have resumed my retreat. Let me introduce you to Col. Clardy and Mr. Jones."

Our friends piloted us across the creek, and gave us directions how and where to go for the night. When we reached the farm house it was nearly dark. When we told the gentleman we were sent there by Col. Clardy to spend the night, we were invited to come in, and were treated like lords. This gentleman gave us some good suggestions and advice and drew us a diagram of the road for thirty miles, to guide us next day.

We started early next morning, and only stopped once to dine. Just before sunset we reached the village, the end of our diagram and day's journey. We were tired and worn out. The man proved to be an old friend and acquaintance of Capt. Gannaway, and gave us a hearty welcome. After supper the whole village came in to see the escaped soldiers and ask questions, about the fight, and the troops who were there and were captured.

Next morning we started for Springfield. After riding five miles, we met a man who told us Springfield was in the hands of the Yankees, and he with others were sent out to warn the people to hide their stock and run off their negroes.

"Captain, we will have to change our course and make for the Cumberland."

We rode back to the village, and while consulting with friends, a young man volunteered to guide us across the country to Ashland,[2] on the river, where he thought we

could cross. In a short time our guide was ready, and
we started for Ashland, 17 miles away. Just before reaching the place we came upon twelve of Gen. [John H.]
Morgan's men,[3] who had been cut off by the rapidly
advancing Federals. They seemed to be lounging by the
wayside resting. When asked why they were stopping out
there in the woods, they told us to ride to the top of the
hill, and we would see a sight, and understand the
situation and position we were in.

## *A Lion Among the Tigers*

---◄•►---

When we reached the hill top a grand sight—and a horrible sight to me—burst upon us. Five large transports with a gunboat in tow, and all crowded with blue coats, were strung along one after another, going up the swollen river to Nashville. We gazed upon the scene without speaking for several moments.

"Well, well," said Gannaway sadly, "the world seems to be filled with Yankees. Yankees before us, Yankees behind, Yankees all around us; can our little army meet this host successfully?"

Presently the boats passed up out of sight. One of Morgan's men, who had been sent into town to reconnoiter, blew his whistle and we all rode into the town of Ashland. We found the ferryboat sunk and no chance to cross that swollen river. The town was full of people and they soon gathered round the soldiers and showed a desire to help us in any way they could. While consulting together an old country doctor came up and told us he had a good boat hid out in the back water four miles below, and if we would go with him, he would put us over the river early next morning.

That night was spent with the good, loyal people of Cheatham county, Tennessee. Next morning at the blast of a horn we met at a designated point and commenced the hard job of crossing the river. For the first time my mule showed his mulishness, and positively refused to go on the boat. Consequently I had to exchange with the doctor who had an old easy going horse. The doctor offered me forty dollars to boot, but I told him the mule had been given me by Col. Clardy, near Clarksville, if he could send him the forty dollars to do so. The boat could only carry three men and their horses, one man held the horses and the other two acted as boatmen. The first who crossed were ordered to push out south, and learn all we could in regard to the Yankees. I shipped on the first load but it required an effort to tackle that raging river again. By 2 p.m. we were all over, and closing up the column we camped that night about fifteen miles from Franklin, Tennessee. Starting early next morning our ears were soon greeted with the sound of Artillery in the direction of Nashville, which caused us to spur up and ride a little faster. About twelve o'clock, noon, we entered the town[1] and found it in a wild state of excitement. The Cavalry had been fighting all the morning on the road to Nashville. Gen. Johnston's[2] army was moving south, and the place would soon be evacuated. I rode immediately to the depot, and found a train just starting south. Turning my old horse loose I boarded the train.

As we moved south a company of soldiers aboard burned the bridges as we passed over. This was slow work and slow traveling, and it was eight o'clock when we reached Columbia.[3] Finding the train would remain two hours I walked up into the city and found it swarming with men and officers of Johnston's retreating army. Walking into a hotel I told the clerk I was an escaped prisoner from Donelson, was out of money and wanted supper on the credit of the Confederacy.

"Walk right in to the table, sir," showing me the dining room, "and when you finish call at the office."

This clerk was dressed in Confederate gray, with lieutenant's stripes or I would never have said what I did, I wished to test him.

On returning to the office, I was furnished with a roll of cigars that lasted me home. Starting at 10 o'clock the train reached Decatur, Ala.,⁴ about 3 p.m.

As the train on the Charleston Railroad thundered up to the depot the guards on the platform sang out:

"No passengers permitted on this train!"

Just then I cared very little for orders, so watching my chance I eluded the guard and entered the car, which I found filled with the roughest looking Irish soldiers I had ever met, the sixth Louisiana regiment, called at home and in Virginia, "Tigers." They had reenlisted for the war, and received a thirty days' furlough and they were going home in a body to enjoy it. One of the roughest, knife in hand and half drunk, approached me as I entered the car and demanded:

"What in the h—l are you doing on this car?"

"Comrade, I heard the order not to enter this car, but I am a soldier, was captured at Donelson, made my escape and I am trying to reach home to refit for the war."

"The h—l you say, come back, comrade, have a drink, and tell us of the 'foit'."

I found Donelson a touchstone to every heart, even the "Tigers." After gratifying their desire in regular Munchausen style, all hands had to drink again, and every one shake hands with me.

I was a lion among the "tigers."

Then this brawny son of Erin said to me:

79

"Aint you tired and schlapy, comrade?"

"Very," said I, "I have not closed my eyes during the night."

"Then, begorra, lie down here on me blanket and go to schlape, and Pat Mahone will guard yez 'til mornin'."

- I was soon fast asleep and slept until the train reached Iuka, where the shouting of Confederate soldiers—Gen. Johnston's advance guard taking position on the ground where the great battle of Shiloh was soon to be fought, won, and lost—aroused me from my slumbers. I looked out at the jolly boys in gray, hoping to see some familiar face but was disappointed. As the train was moving off a soldier recognized me, and running to the rear car told Capt. Allen Stokes[5] I was on board. In a few minutes Capt. Stokes, an old friend from Hernando, Miss., came through the car hunting me, and together we returned to the rear car to meet other old friends. While talking to them and telling the old story, a splendidly dressed staff officer came up and listened attentively to the end. Slapping me on the shoulder, he said:

"You must report to Gen. [Daniel] Ruggles at Corinth."

"Is the General's headquarters near the depot, Captain? I must go on to Memphis on this train, for I have no money, blankets or clothing, and I must go home and refit."

"Orders are imperative, sir, and you must report," said the Captain, walking out of the car.

"Here, Wilson," said Stokes, handing me his pocket book. "You will need money, help yourself."

"I will take $5, as I want my breakfast."

"Ain't you going to report?"

"Not today."

"How are you going to avoid it? The guard will get you if you leave the train, and we are almost there?"

"Will you assist me?"

"Yes, any way I can."

I wrapped my nubia around his neck, put my cloak around his shoulders and exchanged hats.

"Now when you think I am nearly through eating, walk out and let the Captain capture you, parley with him until you see me pass to the train then show your papers and as the train starts jump aboard."

I ate until the whistle blew, and as I passed rapidly to the train I saw Stokes under guard and talking to the Captain, who looked like he had captured a Yankee instead of a Confederate officer. When Stokes saw me enter the cars he told the officer he had made a mistake, and showed his pass and orders.

"Ain't you from Donelson," said the Captain.

"No sir. I am from Iuka."

"Where in the h—l is that Donelson fellow?"

"He has gone to report," said Stokes as he stepped aboard the train.

He came into the car laughing. So we sped on toward Memphis. My story is nearly ended. I am nearing home.

To avoid the guard at the Charleston depot I determined to jump from the train as it slowed up on Union street. I took my stand on the lower step and awaited "orders" from Capt. Stokes to "jump." The whistle sounded, the speed slackened, the order was given and I sprang into the street and was home again!

L. J. WILSON,

1st Lt. Co. F. 1st Miss. Rgt.

I started up Union street at a brisk walk. All at once the idea occurred to me, where am I going? Whom do I seek? Is my wife and child in the city? Has she been able to stand the excitement and suspense of the past month? Has my dear old father been able to stand the strain upon his old system, burdened with its three score and ten years? Such thoughts crowded rapidly through my brain, and produced a strang revulsion of feeling. I began to feel very strangely, my legs grew weak and tremulous, and seemed about ready to refuse to perform duty. I had a presentment of something horrible awaiting me. I was about to come to a standstill and sit down on the sidewalk. Fortunately a cab came rapidly down the street, and stopping a block away, some ladies alighted, and as the driver closed the door and started for his box, I beckoned to him to hold. As I came up he opened the door and politely helping me in, asked:

"Are you sick, sir?"

"No," I answered, "I don't think I am. Please drive me to No. —— Front street, to Sampson, Hayes & Co."[6]

I knew I would find my nephew, Adrian Howze,[7] who was their bookkeeper, who could tell me all I wanted to know, and relieve my anxiety. When I entered the office, Col. Hayes, who was conversing with a gentleman some distance down the sample room, recognized me, and exclaimed:

"My God, Adrian, look behind you!"

My nephew turned from his desk where he was writing, and when he saw me, clasped me in his strong arms, asking:

"Where did you come from? Are you wounded? Are you sick?"

"No," I said ,"Where is wife and Frank?"

"They are at Peyton Skipwith's."[8]

"Are they well?"

"Yes," he replied.

"How is my old father?"

"In good health. We heard from him yesterday."

"Jim, we thought you were dead," said Col. Hayes shaking my hand, "but what is the matter with you, your hand is cold, and you are pale as a ghost?"

"I guess, Colonel, that I have had a nightmare, or a spell of hysterics, for I am as weak as a cat."

"Hold a minute and I will fix that."

He brought a glass of stiff toddy, and ordered me to swallow it. Accustomed to obeying orders, I did so, and soon began to feel much better.

"Come," I said, "go with me to find my wife. Peyton Skipwith has moved since I was here, and I don't remember where. Have you heard nothing at all of me?"

"Yes, two soldiers reported you dead, and a third said you had been sent to prison."

"Did my wife believe me dead, or a prisoner?"

"No, she never has believed it, and has confidently looked for you to come in every day."

"Well come along and go with me, we will find her."

And now I will stop right here. There are some things too sacred to be written, some scenes in this life that angels alone must witness.

The next day I went up into the city and had the pleasure of meeting many friends I had not seen in months. I met with fathers whose sons were in prison who had been in Memphis for days hoping to hear something definite in regard to them. Some of them I could comfort, others I could not.

I had the pleasure to meet Maj. Severson,[9] General

Alcorn's Quartermaster, who paid me for six months service in the Confederate army.

I soon had a new uniform, two good blankets and an oil cloth and was ready for the field again.

After spending two or three days most pleasantly with my Memphis kin and friends, I started with my wife and baby for the old homestead in Desoto County, Mississippi.[10] It was a great pleasure to meet my dear old father and kindred, but it was a bitter pill to meet and face the fathers and mothers of the brave boys I had enlisted six months before and carried into the army.

For several days I did nothing but talk, talk and tell of the siege and surrender, and answer questions in regard to boys now in prison on Johnson's Island and in Camp Chase. But the excitement and mortification of this disaster soon wore away and was swallowed up by the military movements that in a short time culminated in the great battle of Shiloh.[11]

I secured thirty recruits in a short time to fill out the unexpired term of the Alcorn Rifles, my old company, and repaired with them to Corinth, Miss., and reported for duty. Reorganization of the army was rapidly progressing under the Act of the Confederate Congress, recently passed, and no recruits or volunteers were received for a shorter period than three years, or the war.[12] This was a stunner to myself and my thirty recruits. I found about 100 men and ten or twelve officers of my old regiment, the 1st Mississippi, and suppose the other regiments in the brigade were similarly represented.

All the refugees from Fort Donelson were turned over to Gen. James R. Chalmers[13] to be reorganized, and the General found he had a hard job on his hands. But he seemed to be doing all he could to satisfy both men and officers. The men were giving little trouble, but the officers were reluctant to resign. I waited a few days to see what would be accomplished, desiring to do the best I could for the men. I could see but one way out of the trouble. My recruits were becoming restive, and I determined to end their suspense and my own. I called upon Gen. Chalmers and said to him:

"My recruits are grumbling, and I am afraid they will think that I have deceived them, and I intend to end the trouble today, and I am anxious to do the right thing, so if you have any advice, give it to me, if you please."

"Will your men enlist for three years?" he asked.

"I think so, General. I have been talking to them on that line, and I believe they will."

Said he: "I will give them and yourself a furlough for thirty days, and you can go home and raise a company for the war."

My men were pleased with the proposal, and in thirty minutes we were sworn into the Confederate service for the war. My resignation as First Lieut. Co. F. 1st. Miss. Reg's, was sent up to headquarters, and returned approved, and my connection with that gallant regiment dissolved, and we started home, enthused with the idea of raising a company for "the war."[14]

# XIV

## On to Richmond

⚊◄◆►⚊

With 30 men, recruits I had carried up to Corinth, to fill out the unexpired term of my old company in the 1st Miss. regiment, I was mustered into service by Brig. Gen. James R. Chalmers, for three years, or the war, and we were given a furlough for 30 days, to go home and raise a company for the war. This was in the latter part of April, 1862.

We started home enthused with the idea. We felt like we had taken a step forward. We felt more like we were soldiers. We were in for the war, let it last one, three or five years. And what now? Faithfulness, energy, loyalty may shorten the contest. My friend and neighbor, Robert W. Locke, united with me in raising the company,[1] and in less than a month we had sworn in about 100 men, and two boys about 13 years old, whose friends desired us to receive and take with us, as both had threatened to run off, and they knew we would take care of them and favor them in every possible way.

When we met to organize, Rob't W. Locke[2] was elected Captain; L. J. Wilson, M.D., 1st Lieutenant; George Adrian Howze,[3] 2nd Lieutenant; Matthew Jones,[4] 3d Lieutenant. Non-Commissioned Officers: Martin Adkins,[5] 1st Sergeant; Wirt Thompson, 2d Sergeant; Henry Smith, 3d Sergeant; John Bowden, 4th Sergeant.

Upon reporting to the Government for duty, we were ordered to Grenada, Miss. On account of bad water and its scarcity, we were ordered up to Oxford, where we were joined in a short time by nine other companies from the northern half of the state, and organized the 42d Miss. regiment,[6] by electing Judge Hugh R. Miller,[7] Pontotoc county, Colonel; Dr. Hillery Moseley,[8] Panola county, Lieutenant Colonel; Wm. Feeney,[9] Desoto county, Major; L. P. Cooper, Panola county, Quartermaster; B. F. Jones,[10] Carroll county, Commissary; J. M. Rossel,[11] M.D., Desoto county, Surgeon; R. L. Taggart,[12] Marshall county, Assistant Surgeon; Oliver Carr,[13] Pontotoc county, Adjutant.

Orders came in a short time for the regiment to report at Richmond, and we had a long, hot, tiresome trip, made mostly on box cars. At Mobile half the regiment were sent up the Alabama river on a boat, the others crossed over the bay and made the trip on the cars. We waited at Montgomery a day or so for the boat, then on cars we proceeded across the states of Alabama and Georgia to Augusta, thence to Kingston, S. C., Wilmington, N. C. and on north to Richmond.[14]

At Montgomery I was detailed, as usual, to stop with some sick men, with orders to cure them up and bring then on as soon as possible. This was lucky for me, for I had time to rest up and take in the city, visiting the places of note, the capital of Alabama, and the first capital of the Confederate States. I had the pleasure of standing where his excellency, Jefferson Davis took the oath of office as President of the Confederate States. I sat in the stand where he delivered his inaugural address, and imbibed deep draughts of southern patriotism, as I listened to a description of the scenes of that day by a brilliant southern lady, who was present at that time, and who escorted me over the building and grounds.

Hurrying forward with my convalescents, I reached Richmond a few days after the discomfiture of McClellan in his "On to Richmond."[15] The great battle had been fought and won, and the Grand Army of the Potomac that was in sight of the church spires of Richmond, when Stonewall Jackson burst upon their right flank and rear at Mechanicsville were huddled up shattered and demoralized in Turkey Bend on James river, thirty miles below the city, saved from utter annihilation by their terrible fleet of gunboats.[16] But the city was safe, and the only evidence of an enemy anywhere, was the occasional roar of one of the big guns of the Federal fleet.

I found our regiment quartered in Camp Lee,[17] some two miles southeast of the capital building, which I suppose was about the center of the city. Camp Lee was a beautiful place, and was used as fair grounds before the war. A plank fence ten feet high enclosed the grounds and buildings, some six acres or more. This was shaded with natural and ornamental trees, and covered with a dense growth of beautiful bluegrass. A fine place for the tired soldiers to lounge around and rest after their long journey.

After resting for several days our regiment was called upon to perform provost guard duty in the city. A Lieutenant with twenty men was sent to the Provost Marshal's office every morning, and relieved at 6 p.m.

One evening on dress parade Co. F, my own company, was ordered to furnish the provost guard the next day. Next morning when the orderly reported my detail

88

ready, I found Albert Norfleet[18] and John Carmichael,[19] our two 13 year old boys in line, with their guns and accoutrements as bright as they could make them, and as proud of their arms as any young urchin of his first bird gun. We were soon assigned to our posts, guarding four different crossings of its streets, with orders to halt every man, and if he failed to have a pass from General Lee, to send him to the provost marshal. John and Albert were placed at the nearest post in full view of the relief guard, who had taken advantage of some shade trees where we had stacked our arms, and sat down on the edge of the pavement to while away the hot June hours. The boys were not more than one hundred yards from us.

About 11 o'clock, one of the men exclaimed, "the boys have captured a man, Lieutenant."

Looking up, horror of horrors, I recognized President Davis. Snatching up my sword I hurried to the scene. This colloquy occurred between Mr. Davis and the boys:

"Have you orders to stop the President on the streets."

Boys: "We were ordered to halt every man, and see that he had a pass from General Lee."

"Where are you from, boys?"

"Mississippi, sir. We belong to the 42d Miss."

"My God!" said Mr. Davis. "Is Mississippi sending her boys to the front?"

"No, sir. All the men were going to the front, and we could not stay at home."

"Well, boys," said Mr. Davis, "always obey orders, and you will make good soldiers."

I arrived on the ground, and not knowing what to do or say, I saluted the President with all the grace I could command, and began to clear my throat and try to speak. Mr. Davis seemed to understand my embarrassment and advancing with that fascinating smile peculiar to the man, said pleasantly:

"Your boys have captured me, Lieutenant, and you will have to release me."

I hardly knew what I said to the President, but I think I said something like this:

"I am sorry you were interrupted in your walk, Mr. Davis, but I am glad I have had the pleasure of meeting you again."

I am sure I said something of the kind as we walked down the street to my guard who were in line, and at my command presented arms. Mr. Davis shook hands with every one, asking after their welfare, where we were quartered, etc., then gracefully saluting, walked on down the street. After going a short distance he stopped, and turning said:

"Can you spare me those boys for an hour, Lieutenant?"

"Certainly, Mr. Davis."

"Please send them over to my residence," he said, pointing to a handsome building down and across the street.

I saw my boys had made a mash on the President and I felt proud of them. I ordered two of the men to go and relieve the boys and send them down to me. The men went up rubbing their eyes and said:

"Boys, the Lieutenant wants you. I am afraid you have played the d——l as he is going to send you to the President, and I expect he will have you shot, good-bye."

The boys came down to me looking a little sheepish and uncertain as to what was coming. I said to them:

"Boys, the President wants you to come over to his mansion," pointing it out, "I suppose to dine with him. I wish I could go with you, for I know you will have a good time. Go now and remember you are Mississippians."

I think they were met at the door by Mr. Davis himself and ushered into the mansion.

Two hours later they came out, flushed with excitement and pleasure. They had dined with the President and Mrs. Davis, and were happy. It was an epoch in their young lives. Those boys, whose names were Albert Norfleet and John Carmichael, lived through the bloody war. They were baptised at Gettysburg and surrendered at Appomattox. They won the badges of veterans.

This was the first and only time those boys ever saw the President. And it was the last time that the writer ever looked upon his manly form, or felt the pressure of his hand. And this reminds me of another scene which occurred years before and which I desire to place on record. The Hon. Jefferson Davis was a candidate for the United States Senate. All the candidates for state offices were to speak in Oxford, Miss. An immense old fashioned barbecue had been prepared by the people, and the great table had been built in the shape of a V, the peculiar form into which Col. Davis threw his regiment to receive the charge of Santa Anna's cavalry on the bloody field of Buena Vista. Mr. Davis reached the hotel in Oxford (The Butler House) on the stage coach an hour earlier than was expected. News of his arrival soon spread over the town and an immense crowd soon gathered around the hotel and began to shout for "Jeff Davis."

A window in the second story was raised and the Hon. Jefferson Davis appeared at this window and we looked upon his graceful, handsome form for the first time in life. He made a ten minute speech. I was but a youth then, I am an old man now, but the closing sentence of that speech I have never forgotten: "Fellow citizens, I have been with you in war, I have been with you in peace, and you may rest assured, I will stand by you in adversity."

Did the man keep his promise! Let his people answer.

# Second Manassas and Sharpsburg

———————◆———————

Pretty soon we were called upon for a heavy detail to guard the Federal prisoners on Belle Island,[1] those who had been captured in the great battles around Richmond. Guarding prisoners we found a very disagreeable duty. The guard went with two days cooked rations, and were on duty forty-eight hours, were then relieved, and were off duty seventy hours, which made it heavy duty. Fortunately this did not last very long, for an exchange of prisoners was affected, and we had the pleasure of guarding them down to Varina landing, twelve miles below Richmond, where they were taken on board the Federal transports and taken north. This was such a remarkable trip I think it worth describing.

The regiment was called on for three hundred men to guard and escort the prisoners, about 5,000 in number, under command of Lt. Col. Moseley.[2] We reached Belle Island about 8 o'clock a.m. About ten the gate was thrown open and the Federal soldiers marched out by fours, and started on the road at quick time. When the last of the column marched out the head was over a mile away and the prisoners almost in a run.

It was the latter part of July and the sun was shining in all its southern fierceness, and the result was many prostrations from the intense heat. About a dozen of our men succumbed, but no deaths among them. Eight or ten of the Federal soldiers dropped and almost instantly expired, and were buried by the road side. The prisoners could hardly be controlled, and a guard had to be placed in front to keep them from walking too fast.

Had this precaution been taken in the morning probably no death would have occurred, for all the cases of sun stroke occurred during the final four miles. The prisoners were then forced to halt and rest for an hour and then, with a guard in front, proceeded slowly on their way without further casualties, and reached the landing about sunset. Turning over the prisoners to the Federal officers we marched back a mile or more to a brook of cool pure water and bivouacked for the night. That is we ate our cold rations by the light of the stars, bathed our dusty faces in the babbling brook, and hunting for a soft place on the ground, curled up for the night, repeating our mother's lullaby:

> "Lord keep us safe this night,
> Secure from all our fears,
> May angels guard us while we sleep,
> 'Till morning light appears."

At daylight we were roused from our virtuous couches, hastily finished our two days rations and fell into line. When we reached the city we found it in a state of excitement over the dispatch from Gen. Jackson, who had been sent north by Gen. Lee to check the advance of Pope, who was marching on to Richmond with another Grand Army. He had issued a ridiculous and bombastic order (when taking command of his army) in regard to his foe. He expected to see only the backs of his enemies, had no rear to his Grand Army. His headquarters would be in the saddle, and he would ride into Richmond in thirty days.[3]

Alas! alas! "The best laid schemes of mice and men, aft gang aglee."

He would have succeeded had there been no obstacles in his pathway, but just before he reached the Rapidan he found an old Virginia Stonewall and a very steep Hill right across his pathway. He pressed forward expecting, or hoping, to see the back of his enemies, but found he had to look Lee's veterans squarely in the face, and the result was a brilliant Confederate victory at Cedar Mountain.[4]

Gen. Longstreet, who had been watching for weeks the embarking of McClellan's army from Turkey Bend on James river, was sending forward his brigades to the support of Jackson as fast as he thought it prudent for the safety of Richmond. These gallant men, as they marched through the city on their way north to meet the enemy, enthused every one who came out to greet and cheer them, and the whole city turned out en masse to bid them God Speed!

Glorious soldiers! How our hearts burned within us to join them on the march. But the 42d Miss. regiment was not yet ready to take the field, and we were just now battling with measles, mumps and camp fever, passing through the acclimating process, the bane of all new or fresh regiments.

Richmond was really the drilling ground of the Confederacy. As fast as the regiments were raised at home, they were hurried off to Richmond, for while drilling and preparing for service, they could be used for defense in case of an attack from a bold force of the enemy's cavalry. Something that happened more than once, and in this way a considerable garrison was kept in and around the city for its defense and safety.

As soon as Longstreet reached him, or drew sufficiently near, Gen. Jackson commenced that celebrated flank movement around Pope's army to Manassas Junction, where he burned Pope's depot of supplies, amounting in value to millions of dollars.[5] After destroying all he could not utilize or carry away, Gen. Jackson marched his army on the plains of Manassas where the first great battle of the war was fought in July 1861, and placing his army in line of battle immediately in Pope's rear, between him and Washington, boldly waited an attack from Pope, whose army outnumbered Jackson 4 to 1. This was indeed a bold act, almost a rash act, but the General knew his men, and the men knew their General, and were not afraid.

Longstreet was pressing on with all possible haste to the support of Jackson, and on the second day of the contest, just in the nick of time burst through Thoroughfare Gap, fell suddenly upon Pope's flank, who was hotly engaged with Jackson, and swept him from the field.[6] Another great victory was added to the Confederate list.

Pope was crushed, and his army, melting away in the direction of Washington, never halting for food or rest until safe within the fortifications of the Capital. After securing the rich fruits of this great battle, Gen. Lee pressed forward to the Potomac, and boldly crossed into Maryland, sending one corps to the left to capture Harper's Ferry with its rich stores and garrison of 12,000 men, which Gen. Jackson accomplished with little or no loss, while Longstreet and Hill held the passes in the mountains of Maryland against the advancing Federals, again under the command of McClellan.

As soon as Harper's Ferry surrendered, Gen. Lee passed through the mountain passes, and concentrated his

army on the west bank of the Antietam river, near Sharps-
burg, where he was attacked by the overwhelming forces
of the enemy, on the 17th of September.[7] This was one
of the hottest, bloodiest battles of the war, and considered
a drawn battle.

Gen. Lee remained in line of battle all of the 18th,
hoping McClellan would attack again, but the gauge of
battle was declined, and our army was quietly withdrawn
to the south bank of the Potomac. I did not intend to give
an account of any military movement in which my own
regiment was not engaged, but seeing Lee's veterans
march through Richmond on their way north to meet the
enemy, and having had such a burning desire to go with
them, I hope I will be pardoned for this condensed account
of this brilliant campaign.

A season of rest followed this summer of battles, and
the Army of Northern Virginia was quartered, each corps
in supporting distance, in a line extending from Winchester, Va., east to Culpeper Court House, with the argus-
eyed Stuart on the flanks. Here we will leave them to
rest and watch the enemy, and return to our own regiment
at Richmond.

# XVI

## Fredericksburg Interlude

———◆———

The cool days and nights of an early autumn were having their invigorating effect upon the men. Measles and mumps disappeared, the camp fever subjects who had been furloughed home to get well, were returning fat and slick for duty. Col. Miller had succeeded in getting his entire regiment uniformed and otherwise equipped, and we were now pretty well drilled, and ready for active service, and were getting anxious to see it.

The city newspapers began to hint at another "On to Richmond" at an early day. From what point would it start? This subject was discussed and guessed at by officers and men, and even by the papers. The river or peninsula route had been tried by the Young Napoleon.[1] The direct or overland route had been tried by Pope and McDowell at the first. McDowell reached Manassas, and Pope was turned back before he reached the Rapidan, or covered half the distance, and now who will be the fourth victim, and from what point would he start?

About 7 o'clock one morning, a courier rode up to headquarters and handed Col. Miller an order:

"Five companies fifty men each."

They were wanted instanter to go to Fredericksburg to guard the fords until Gen. Lee's army arrived. This sounded like business, and sent a thrill of pleasure through every heart. So the problem is partly solved, the "On to

Richmond" will be via Fredericksburg.[2] We were ordered to be at the depot by 2 p.m., with two days cooked rations. Excitement reigned supreme. Every officer and man was anxious to get to Lee's army. We were tired of Richmond, tired of guard duty, tired of camp. We wanted to see active service, wanted to be numbered with the veterans. At 1 o'clock we were ordered into line. Every man and officer was in his new uniform, and guns and accoutrements as bright as silver dollars. Maj. Feeney, who was placed in command, was proud of his battalion. We made the run in two hours, and were put off the cars in the outskirts of the city, as the engineer was afraid to go to the depot for fear of being fired on.

We met with a warm reception by the good people of Fredericksburg. The ladies and old men, in fact the entire population was on the sidewalks to greet and welcome us. "God bless you, boys!" "God bless you, boys!" was heard on every side, as they pressed forward to shake our hands, and many of the ladies were weeping hysterically. It was a heart stirring scene and a welcome one, and I doubt not that every man in that battalion of Mississippians would have died at the fords we were placed to defend had the Federals advanced upon us.

The Federals occupied the heights beyond the Rappahannock,[3] and had two or three pieces of Artillery leveled on the town in a menacing manner, and their Cavalry would ride down to the river in squads of four or five to water their horses, but made no attempt to cross, and when our boys would raise their guns as if they intended to fire, they would point to their Artillery as much as to say:

"Shoot if you dare, and we will shell your town."

99

Thus affairs stood for twenty-four hours, when Col. Ball, of the 9th Va. Cavalry, came to the rescue, and for two or three days played a regular game of bluff, showing his regiment at different places, and blowing his bugle calls at different points. He made us believe that we had a whole division of Stuart's Cavalry to back us, and we felt very brave, and it is probable the enemy thought the same thing, at least they made no effort to cross the river, and we were perfectly satisfied.

On the morning of the second day, an order was received at headquarters, requesting that all the officers and men off duty would assemble in the public park at 1 p.m. and partake of refreshments prepared by the ladies of Fredericksburg. We were all there on time, about 100 of us, the balance were at their posts up and down the river. The Mayor made a beautiful and appropriate speech, welcoming the Mississippians to old Virginia, and thanking us for coming to their defense in the hour of danger, etc., really making us feel like we had performed some great service, preventing the capture of the city.

When the Mayor closed, we called upon Capt. A. M. Nelson,[4] of Co. A., who, by the time the Mayor closed his pleasant and complimentary speech, was full to the brim, stepped out, and made one of the handsomest speeches and appropriate replies I ever heard on any occasion. We were proud of our orator.

While the speech making was going on the mothers, God bless them, with the assistance of the old Virginia darkies, were spreading their table cloths on the grass, and loading them with the good things of the Old Dominion. The young ladies, the beauties of the city, were talking familiarly and pleasantly with us, like old friends and acquaintances, and we really felt we were among friends and enjoying a grand old picnic at home. And what a dinner! The recollection of the good things makes my mouth grow moist, after the lapse of forty years. We were all enjoying the society of the ladies as much or more than the luxuries of that table, especially the young unmarried soldiers.[5] That beau ideal of a bachelor and ladies man of the Regiment, Capt. Jno. Powell,[6] was in the zenith of his glory, with a Virginia beauty on each side dispensing the good things of those tables, he could hardly take time to talk, but he was smiling all over the top of his bald pate. The enemy upon the heights, could look down on us and with their field glasses, which we could see they were using, understanding exactly what we were doing, and I wonder what impressions were made upon them. We lingered as long as possible around that table with those good people, but the pleasant scene, and hour, must pass, we shake hands, bid adieu and part, never to meet again. In a few hours Lee's veterans relieved us, and we were ordered back to camp at Richmond.

Truly there are green spots along the soldier's pathway, and we had enjoyed one of them.[7]

# XVII

## The Author Becomes Assistant Surgeon

———————◆•◆———————

When we returned to camp we found everything in statu quo, the cool fine autumn weather was building up the convalescents. Surgeon Rossel had recovered from his spell of fever, had sent in his resignation, and would start home as soon as it was returned accepted. Col. Miller would, and did appoint Dr. Taggart[1] Surgeon, and I at last had a chance for the position of Assistant Surgeon. I had been on duty as Assistant Surgeon for more than two months and I felt that I had a right to contest for the position. I met with considerable opposition from my Colonel, but I had the Lieutenant-Colonel, Major and all the company officers to back me, and went to work for the position, and succeeded in about a month in getting an order from the Secretary of War to appear before Gen. Lee's Medical Examining Board for examination for the position.[2] Having passed a satisfactory examination I was ordered to report to Medical Director Cullen,[3] Richmond, for assignment. Dr. Cullen wanted to assign me to one of the city hospitals, but I prevailed on him to assign me to the 42d Miss. Regiment, and I was happy.

The regiment was now a part of the force guarding the Capital, the garrison of Richmond. We were moved south of the James, midway between Richmond and Petersburg, near the railroad, so as to be in easy range of either city or Drury's Bluff,[4] as emergencies might require. Here we quietly rested for some time, drilling daily and perfecting ourselves in military tactics.

One evening I was sitting outside my tent in the warm sunshine, reading to while away the weary hours. Raising my eyes and looking down the road toward Petersburg, I saw a fine specimen of the "genus homo" walking briskly up the pike, with a good size grip in one hand and a large or long walking stick in the other. The first thought was, he was some returning soldier, but he soon came near enough for me to discover that he was a negro, over six feet in height, large, stalwart form, and hair and beard nearly white. I became interested, and in a few moments was astonished at receiving a courtly, graceful military salute from the old man.

"Won't you stop and rest awhile, and tell me where you are going, Uncle?"

"Thank you, sir, I will, for I am a little tired from my walk. I am on my way to Richmond, and from there I will go on to my old home near Lexington, where I was born more than eighty years ago."

"How long have you been away from home, Uncle?"

"Nearly fifty years, sir."

"Goodness! Where have you been all those years?"

"Away out west, sir, acting as government interpreter among the Indians."

My astonishment increased. Here was a most interesting United States government official. An old veteran soldier who had been in service fifty years. Of course my curiosity was aroused to learn his history, and this is what I learned. He had been with Gen. Andrew Jackson in the Creek war, and was in the terrible battles of Talledega, Muckaw and Horseshoe Bend, where the Creek Indians were overpowered and brought to terms, and the old soldier gave me a graphic account of those terrible conflicts with the redmen, and many thrilling incidents during the Indian wars. He loved to talk of General Jackson and General Coffee. When the Indians were moved west into the Territory, he went with the troops that accompanied them, and had been with them ever since.

When he heard that war had occurred between the North and the South, instanter he wanted to come home, back to old Virginia. No objection was made to his leaving the fort where he had been for so many years, in fact, I think he had a permit. He had recommendations from Confederate officers in the Trans-Mississippi department, and from ladies and gentlemen asking help for the old man. He had quite a tiresome trip from northwest Texas, across Louisiana and Mississippi to Meridian, where he saw a railroad for the first time in life. Friends bought him a ticket and sent him to Montgomery, Ala., and then he was sent on to Richmond.

I asked him why he got off the cars and walked from Petersburg to Richmond?

"Well, sir," he said: "When the cars stopped at Petersburg, I got out and thought I would walk about a little, I was so tired riding, and I see a sign, 'Fresh Oysters,' and I thought I would like a stew, so I went in and had a mess of oysters, and when I came out the cars were gone."

I sent him over to Richmond in an ambulance next morning, sent him to the Mayor. The next day a very interesting history of the old man was published in the daily papers. In due time he was sent on home to finish his days among his old master's children.

"I'm gwine back to Dixie
And I must go!"

## Winter Quarters

On Dec. 13th Gen [Ambrose E.] Burnside began his "On to Richmond" by bombarding Fredericksburg from Stafford Heights.[1] He was held in check and prevented from laying down his pontoons and crossing, until Lee could arrange his lines, by Barksdale's brigade of Mississippians, who were posted among the buildings along the river bank. When everything was in readiness Barksdale was ordered to fall back and let them come. The Federals crossed over, 113,000 strong, and met with a crushing defeat, losing over 12,000 men killed and wounded.

The only effect this "On to Richmond" had upon my own regiment was a change of base from the south to the lines northeast of the city for a short while. After the excitement of this great battle had subsided, both armies settled down into winter quarters for a season of rest and repose. Our regiment was ordered back to camp south of the city, in time to make ourselves comfortable for the winter, and get ready for Christmas.[2]

This was the jolliest, merriest Christmas we spent during the war. The railroads were all intact, and many boxes of good things were brought from home by returning comrades who had been on sick furloughs, and the lucky man always divided his good things and the 42d Miss. had been in and around Richmond so long the boys knew all the avenues of ingress and egress, and could get anything they wanted.

Rations were good and plentiful, and every one had Confederate money, and it was worth a good deal. Turkeys, chickens, eggs, and even old Virginia apple brandy could be had at reasonable figures, and there was no reason why we should not have a merry Chrismas, and we had it, and enjoyed it like good soldiers.[3]

About the first of February we were hustled aboard the cars, and sent south to Goldsboro, N. C., to protect our railroad communications, which were threatened by a raid from the coast up the river.[4] The raid was repulsed at Newbern by the time we reached Goldsboro, and we had our trip for nothing. We remained at Goldsboro for nearly a week, and then marched through the country via Tarboro to Weldon, where we boarded the cars, and went to Blackwater river, to guard that line against a raid to the rear of Richmond and Petersburg. This running around to find or meet the enemy was becoming monotonous, and the men were growing restive, and anxious to use their arms a little. They wanted to shoot. They seemed to be actually spoiling for a fight.

A splendid wooden bridge spanned the Blackwater, a small but deep stream, which flowed into the Roanoke, a large stream half a mile below the bridge. Our regiment guarded this bridge. Rifle pits were already dug, and a considerable force were on duty day and night, with a picket half a mile in advance down the Suffolk road. There we were quartered for some time, and enjoyed the shad season. There was a fishing place on the Roanoke, a half mile away, and when it was put into operation, it was quite a show to Mississippians. Officers had difficulty in keeping the men in camp. We had been accustomed to haul out a dozen or so at a time when we went seining at home, but when we saw an old mule drag out at one haul more big, shining, flapping shad, weighing from one to six pounds each, than six big mules could pull on wheels, the seining became intensely interesting, and they tickled our stomachs.

We enjoyed these fine fish until Gen. Longstreet ordered an advance on Suffolk, and closely invested that place about April 1st, pressing up closely around the formidable works of the enemy, as though he intended to storm the place.[5] The bloodthirsty 42d began to think their desire for a fight would soon be gratified, but they were doomed to disappointment. The movement was made for a double purpose, first to draw off a part of the formidable force in Lee's front at Fredericksburg, under the brave Gen. [Joseph] Hooker, who boasted that he commanded the finest army on the planet, and enable Gen. Lee to meet that army successfully on the fatal field of Chancellorsville, but secondly and chiefly to collect and secure the immense amount of provisions in the southeast counties of the State, which our army would need during the summer campaign. The amount of provisions secured was something enormous. Our Regimental Commissary, Capt. B. F. Jones, reported over 100,000 pounds of bacon delivered to the Commissary General, and he was one of fifteen Commissaries collecting these provisions. They also secured flour, wheat and corn, and tons upon tons of hay for the Cavalry. Capt. Jones distinguished himself in this work, and secured promotion for his efficiency and zeal, and Maj. Jones was ordered to Mississippi in the fall, to collect the "tax in kind" imposed upon the farmers of the South by Congress to support our armies in the field.[6]

Both objects having been accomplished, Gen. Longstreet fell back to the Blackwater, then to Petersburg and Richmond.[7] We were now placed in a brigade with the 2d and 11th Miss. veteran regiments, 55th N. C., and 48th Ala., battalion, making altogether a very handsome brigade of 2,500 or 3,000 muskets, and placed under command of Brig. Gen. Jos. R. Davis, a nephew of our beloved President.[8] We were soon en route to Fredericksburg, and were assigned to the division of Maj. Gen. H. Heth,[9] and the 3d Army Corps, commanded by the fiery A[mbrose Powell] Hill.[10] As a regiment we were where we had longed to be for months. We were at last in a fine place to see service, and we saw it.[11]

# Invasion of Pennsylvania

Gen. Joe Hooker commenced his "On to Richmond" early in May, 1863, with probably greater prospects of success than any of his predecessors. He boasted that he commanded the finest army on the planet. In equipment, discipline and efficiency it was perfect, and the field returns show that his army numbered 138,378 present on April 30th. Gen. Lee had 53,303, and yet Hooker met with a more disastrous defeat than any of them, unless it was Burnside.

But the loss of Gen. Jackson counter-balanced all the advantages and trophies of the battle of Chancellorsville. A great man had fallen, and every soldier in the army of Northern Virginia felt it, and no one felt it more keenly than the commanding General. When told, by his aide, that Gen. Jackson had lost his left arm, it is said Gen. Lee bowed his head for a moment, and in deepest emotion said:

"Go and tell Gen. Jackson that I have lost my right arm!"

A glorious tribute to a noble soldier!

A gloom for a while settled over the army, and over the entire people of the South. But as our great leader began to concentrate his scattered forces, and the objects of the campaign became apparent to the people and the army, a wave of enthusiasm spread from center to circumference, and the grandest army the Confederacy ever mustered followed Lee from Fredericksburg to the rich fields of Pennsylvania.

Gen. Joe Hooker was too strongly posted on Stafford Heights to be attacked by Gen. Lee with any prospects of success, without too great a loss of human life. The position was naturally a very strong one, and everything that engineering skill could devise had been done to render it impregnable.[1] So Gen. Lee determined to try and maneuver Hooker out of his strong position.

About June 9th Lee started [Richard Stoddert] Ewell,[2] who was in command of Jackson's famous corps, on to Winchester, where on June 14th, just five days after leaving Fredericksburg he routed [General Robert Huston] Milroy, capturing several thousand prisoners, twenty-eight pieces of artillery and an immense amount of quartermaster and commissary stores. Securing these Ewell boldly crossed the Potomac and pressed on to Yorktown, Penn. This bold and sudden movement produced consternation in Washington and all over the North, and "Fighting Joe" was suddenly called to defend the National Capital. As soon as Hooker started for Washington, Hill's corps filed out of the ditches in front of Fredericksburg, and following Longstreet, who was far on the way, made for the Potomac.[3] We marched through a portion of the battlefield of Chancellorsville, and witnessed some of the horrors of war. It had been about six weeks since that terrible battle was fought, and the stench was, in places, perfectly awful. The little hillocks, scattered here and there along the route for several miles, were silent witnesses of the savagery of man, and the horrors of war. These men had been buried hastily, and many of them hardly covered beneath the sod, and here and there an arm or a leg was sticking out, the flesh stripped from the bones by the beasts of the field and the vultures of the air that had congregated in countless numbers to satiate their hunger with human food.

We were glad to pass this horrid field and reach a place where we could quench our thirst, for the evening was very warm, our canteens dry and we had been marching at quick time for several hours. About sunset we went into camp, or bivouac for the night. Fires were soon ablaze, coffee made, and our soldier rations consumed and we were ready for bed. At 2 a.m. the long roll roused us from our virtuous couches, and orders were sent down to move in one hour.

This will serve as the program for the long march to Gettysburg and back. Though after the second day the halt was made about 12 m. and not later than 2 p.m.

We were passing through Culpeper county, a beautiful country of hills and dales, and pure running brooks, fine farm houses and barns, rich lands with a promising crop of wheat and clover. We soon had glimpses of the Blue Ridge range of mountains in the distance, which looked more like a bank of dark clouds, or smoke, low down on the horizon, than a range of mountains, but intensely blue.

The third day of our march we entered Winchester Gap, and camped for the night. My own regiment in a small cove in the mountains covered with a dense growth of red clover, which made a splendid bed for a tired soldier. We were surrounded with mountains that seemed to us, in the gathering darkness of a cloudy evening, to reach the heavens. Here we were permitted to witness a grand scene. A storm had been gathering for some time and we prepared as best we could to take a summer drenching, but fortunately for us very little rain fell, but we had the grandest electrical display we ever witnessed. The peals of thunder were rapid and terrible, and seemed to shake the mountains to their center, and the vivid flashes of lightning, playing up and down the mountain side, were blinding to the eye, and beautiful and grand beyond description. We watched the warring elements until the storm passed over us, and sped on to the east and the rumbling thunder in the distance lulled the tired soldiers to sleep. Early dawn found us struggling up the pass and by noon we rested upon the summit of the mountains and feasted our eyes upon the beautiful valley of the Shenandoah, and the Alleghany mountains in the distance.

Winchester, grand old Winchester, could be seen in the distance, with its church spires pointing to heaven; and villages and hamlets dotted the beautiful landscape, while here and there those mute monuments of the devastating hand of war—lone chimneys—where once stood handsome farm houses, sheltering happy families.

We descended the mountains much easier than we ascended, and crossing the Shenandoah at Front Royal, bore to the right, and by 4 p.m. went into camp in a beautiful grove near the village of Berryville. We were now passing over ground made historic and sacred by the tread of Stonewall Jackson and his foot cavalry in the campaign of 1862, when they immortalized themselves and astonished the world by their rapid movements up and down this valley in pursuit of the enemy.

Early dawn found us on the march, and the impression seemed to be general that we would cross the Potomac, and camp in Maryland tonight. I fell behind from some cause, probably because the troops were marching more rapidly than usual. They seemed to be enthused with the idea of crossing the Potomac and carrying the war into the enemy's country.[4]

About noon, as I rounded a spur in the mountains, the broad Potomac was before me, but at least 200 feet below the point where I stood. The road turned squarely to the right and headed toward the river. The scene which presented itself was enough to arouse enthusiasm in every southern heart. Over the hills beyond the river as far as the eye could reach a line of gray soldiers were marching, cheering as they went, their bright arms glittering in the sunshine. Below at the river the men were marching across, holding their cartridge boxes up to keep them dry. A short distance below the line of men the artillery was crossing, and above, the wagon train and ambulances. Bands were playing Dixie on the Virginia shore and Maryland, My Maryland, beyond the river. The scene was grand and inspiring.

If Gen. Hooker commanded the grandest army on the planet at Chancellorsville, what could Gen. Lee say of this army, if he could descend to compliments?

That night we camped in Maryland. The few citizens we saw along the highway did not seem particularly rejoiced to see us. Occasionally a lady would wave her handkerchief in the house, as if she was afraid to come to the door and show it, and we decided that we would gain very few recruits by liberating Maryland.

The next morning in passing through Greencastle, a considerable town on the way, two or three hundred bright girls came out of a large school or college, and lined the road to see the Rebels pass, and the last mother's daughter had on the United States flag for an apron, and impudently asked the boys if they would not like to fight under it. We were in the enemy's country, and no mistake. This little incident satisfied me in regard to the political status of Maryland.

We pressed on toward Gettysburg, and Friday evening our brigade went into camp on a hill or mountain just above the village of Cashtown, where we rested for two days. Saturday evening on dress parade, Gen. Lee's order was read, requesting all chaplains to hold Divine services on Sabbath day, and if possible administer the communion of the Lord's Supper. That Sabbath day was a high day for us. The sun rose gloriously bright and the day was ushered in, and we were aroused from our slumbers by the band playing—

> "Safely thro' another week
> God has led us on our way," etc.

and an unusual quiet rested upon the camp.

At 11 o'clock the brigade was assembled by the band playing most impressively "Old Hundred." Our beloved chaplain, Rev. T. D. Witherspoon,[5] preached one of his able and most impressive sermons. The Communion services were peculiarly appropriate and comforting to christians, and all availed themselves of this opportunity, probably the last, to enjoy this precious feast. Gen. Lee was present and sitting among his christian soldiers, celebrated with them the death and suffering of our Lord and Savior. What a precious privilege. It was truly a feast of "fat things" to our souls, and we went in the strength of that meal for many days.

# *Gettysburg*

———◆—

Monday morning Davis' brigade was ordered out in a certain direction to protect the Engineers in making a diagram or map of the country for Gen. Lee. I never learned the points of the compass while in Maryland and Pennsylvania, and consequently I cannot say in what direction we marched or fought while in those states. We moved out five or six miles from Cashtown, where we bivouacked for the night, putting out pickets in every direction on the road. The Engineers prosecuted their work rapidly, taking the altitude of the hills and mountains, and drawing maps of the various roads and streams. We were not disturbed, and the Engineers completing their work, Tuesday evening we marched back to our position above Cashtown, having learned that the citizens were very much afraid of the Rebels, closing their doors and blinds as we passed their houses. Not one of them, old or young, came out to talk or speak to us while we camped among them, or as we came back. They thought we were cannibals and might eat their young children, or thought we would be as mean and despicable as their own soldiers when marching through our Southland, and burn and pillage and steal.

Wednesday, July 1st, we were on the road at an early hour, and marched up the Hagerstown pike toward Gettysburg. Davis' brigade was in front. The report was soon spread among the men that we were sent out to find the enemy, and the report proved to be true. After marching three or four miles, we began to meet women and children hastening back, fleeing for their lives, many of them weeping bitterly. It was a sad and touching sight to us, but then it was something our wives and children had been suffering all around our war-girt land for months, and we could only hope that when these people learned something of the horrors of war, it would make them a little more charitable towards their southern neighbors.

Those fleeing women satisfied us we were getting near the enemy, and the men seemed to quicken their pace. We had been ascending a gradual incline for a mile or more. When we reached the top of the hill, or ridge, a beautiful expanse of country lay before us for about a mile and a half, covered with a luxuriant growth of wheat nearly ready for the husbandman's sickle. A little to the right of a direct line was Gettysburg, a beautiful town, and beyond it a high range of hills. This is about what we took in at a glance, but we had little time to admire the beautiful landscape, dotted over with handsome farm houses, and the finest barns I ever saw. There was a puff of smoke a mile away, followed by a loud report, and a shell went hurtling over our heads. Another and another followed in quick succession. The brigade was rapidly deployed into line and advanced across the wheat field toward the battery. We were moving down a gentle declivity to a considerable brooklet that crossed the field diagonally, and we were soon out of reach of the battery.

The enemy's skirmish line was posted along this brooklet, and we soon began to hear the peculiar hiss of the minnie ball. Our skirmishers were rapidly advanced, and the line of battle passed the brook, and advanced at quick time up the incline toward the enemy over the hill. Finding cool, fresh water in the brook, I established my field hospital under some trees, and ordered my litter corps to bring the wounded to that place.[1]

Up to this time only three men had been wounded, but they rapidly increased to more than forty. Our line advanced steadily and rapidly up the hill, and when they reached the crest, found the enemy massed beyond. Instantly the order was given to retreat, and the line fell back in good order to a point far in the rear of my field hospital. I succeeded in getting my wounded all off to the division hospital, and returned to my regiment, which I found lying in line awaiting orders. After talking with the officers and men, and learning all I could in regard to the killed who were left upon the field, I walked to the top of the hill where three pieces of artillery were leisurely firing in the direction of the enemy we had just found. The officer in command of the guns was watching the shells with his field glass, and I heard him say:

"Don't fire quite so high, boys. Gen. Ewell is coming up in the rear of those fellows, and your shells might reach him."

That was news too good to keep, and I returned to my regiment and reported. Our men were not at all satisfied with the morning skirmish, and were glad to learn they might have another chance at the enemy. Dr. Holt proposed that we go to the top of a hill a short distance in the rear, and get a good view of the battle. Obtaining permission, we made for the hill, and before we reached the top the attack commenced and must have been a complete surprise. The Federals (Reynolds' Corps) rushed out of their breastworks into that wheat field, for Gettysburg. That wheat field was more than a mile wide and the Federals maintained no order and seemed to be twenty deep as they passed over the field.

Ewell's line was at right angles to our own, which was ordered forward, and they were soon under a complete cross-fire. The battery on the hill had been increased to eight or ten pieces, and were dropping their shells among the fleeing Yankees as rapidly as they could fire. We could see everything plainly from our hill top, and every shell seemed to bring down a dozen men when it exploded. It was a glorious sight to us then, but horrible to think of at this distant day. The enemy were followed closely by our men into Gettysburg, and a large number of prisoners were captured and marched back through our lines that night, estimated at 6,000 or 7,000.[2]

Near nightfall I was ordered to see that all the dead were buried, and all the wounded sent back to the hospital. This forced me to go all over that horrid field. The Pioneer corps soon came, and I selected a place to bury our dead, when they went to work digging the trenches. My litter corps brought in the dead as rapidly as possible. The poor, wounded Federals were crying piteously for water in every direction. We kept our canteens filled and administered comfort to as many as possible. This was my first experience on the battlefield after the fighting, and it was horrible beyond description. If every human being could have witnessed the result of the mad passions of men as I saw it that night, war would cease, and there would never be another battle. "It must needs be that offenses come, but woe unto that man by whom they come."

It was midnight before we finished our sad task, and turned our weary steps toward the division hospital. Among the dead of the 42d Miss. regiment was my own nephew, Lieut. George Adrian Howze,[3] who was shot in the advance upon the enemy in the morning, or about noon. His faithful servant, Stephen, came out on the battlefield and sought for and found his body, and carried it back to the hospital for burial. My servant Ellick was waiting for me and had my supper ready, which I ate ravenously, as I had not tasted food since early in the morning.[4]

July 2d my cook waked me at sunrise and had breakfast ready. I asked for my Surgeon and found that he was "hors de combat," and that I would have no assistance from him in the treatment and care of the wounded that day. Drs. Hubbard and Ward both kindly proffered all the assistance they could render, and by dark I had all the wounded in pretty good condition, and comparatively comfortable. Longstreet's corps passed our hospital about noon, and by three o'clock attacked the enemy on the extreme right, and drove them back in the direction of Cemetery Ridge. The fighting was terrific, and continued until darkness put an end to the contest.

July 3, 1863 was a memorable day in the history of our country—a memorable day in the history of the army of Northern Virginia. The third act in the great drama of Gettysburg was about to begin. The Federal army was massed on Cemetery Hill and Round Top mountain, and well protected by breastworks and stone fences. Nearly two hundred pieces of artillery were in position to sweep the plain over which the Confederate army must pass to reach those works. The Confederate army was also in posi-

119

tion, Longstreet's corps on the right, Hill in the center and Ewell on the left with 160 pieces of artillery. Toward noon the artillery commenced firing, and for three hours we had pandemonium. Think of three-hundred pieces of artillery firing as fast as the men could load them coupled with the bursting of shells, and possibly you may form an idea of the noise.

The air seemed to be in a state of vibration, and produced a very strange feeling in one's head.

The cannonade over, the order, "Forward," was given, the boys in gray advanced over the hill, and the contest was begun.

I shall not attempt to describe this fierce charge of the Confederates, for abler pens, held by those who were present on the field and eye witnesses of the deeds of daring and heroism enacted that day, have described it.[5] My duties were elsewhere and I returned to my post.

Early in the morning I was ordered to my command. I had been constantly engaged during the previous day and half the night attending to the wounded of the first day's battle, then I slept three hours, hastily ate my breakfast and hurried to the battlefield. I found Holt and Shields waiting for me and, together, started out to find a suitable place for a field hospital. After walking ourselves down, we selected a large barn as the best place we could find for our wounded, with water at hand and plenty of hay and straw for bedding. This was a typical Pennsylvania barn—lower story built of stone. So we had three walls of stone between ourselves and the battlefield, which would protect us against bullets, grape and canister, and here we prepared for the coming storm. And caring for our wounded, which consisted chiefly in extracting bullets, legating bleeding vessels, checking hemorrhages in different ways, splinting fractured limbs so that the poor sufferers could be sent in ambulances, to the real hospital for appropriate treatment. This hospital was usually two or three miles in the rear of the battlefield. To apply the term hospital to this field station was really a misnomer. But here the assistant surgeon got in his ministrations of mercy to the wounded. Often we had the pleasure of saving life by the legation of an artery, or application of the tourniquet. Here often had the sad pleasure of writing down the last messages of love and affection to the dear ones at home, whispering words of consolation and hope into the ears of the dying.

If my old hand does not become too shaky, I will report a case which wrung our hearts with anguish and blinded our eyes from weeping, for many days. The terrible canonade progressing, and increasing every moment as new batteries were brought into action. Several slightly wounded had walked back and had their wounds dressed, when we saw the first litter from the battlefield nearing our station, borne by four stout men; and we knew someone desperately wounded was coming.

Who is it? Who is it?

As they drew near a young soldier raised his head and exclaimed in a clear voice:

"Doctor, they have got Jerry Gage at last. I thought I would go through safely, but they have got me."

"I hope not Jerry," said Dr. Shields in a trembling voice, "I hope not."

"Well, come and help the boys lay me down. Be easy, boys."

"Now, Doctor, examine me and tell me the truth."

A glance at the wound was sufficient to convince us that it was mortal. A piece of shell had struck the left side near the stomach, tearing away the tissues, a rib and the spleen and fractured the left forearm lascerating it terribly.

"Is it mortal?"

"Yes, Jerry, you can't live over that wound."

"How long can I live, Doctor?"

"Three hours, Jerry, maybe longer."

"That is long enough, let me have pen and paper, for I must write to mother and my dear girl before I die."

We placed him as comfortably as possible, a comrade supporting his head and shoulder, and another holding the plank and paper upon which he was writing, and the dying soldier rapidly penned his last messages home. We sat silently looking on. Finishing the first page, he calmly said:

"Turn the paper, John."

As we replaced the paper, he said:

"Let me see, where did I get?"

His mind seemed to be running more rapidly than he could write.

John turned the paper, Jerry looked, and then wrote on. The din of the battle was terrific, the explosions rapid and continued, but the dying soldier heeded it not, but rapidly wrote on, until he had filled three pages of foolscap.

"Doctor," he said, "take this and fold it up for me, and I will continue to write, as I begin to feel very strangely."

We gave him water and brandy, and he continued writing rapidly until he finished his second letter. This he gave to the doctor to fold, and then asked for the letters. He pressed each to his ghastly wound, staining the blank side with his blood.

"Let them dry, doctor, and send them home to Oxford, Miss. Send them by hand if you can, for I don't want them to miscarry. Now I am through. Come around me, boys, and let us talk. I want to look at you as long as I can."

His countenance blanched, a paroxysm of pain shook his frame, and we feared he was going into convulsions, but we gave him chloroform to inhale, and he fell asleep for a while. Rousing up, he said:

"Oh! Doctor, I can't bear that pain. I am dying. Please give me something to prevent it, and let me die easy."

The doctor, with a trembling hand measured out a large dose of morphine in brandy, and gave him to swallow, then after inhaling the chloroform for a few moments he fell asleep and slept for some time. Rousing up, he said:

"Boys, come near me, it's growing dark. I can't see you. Come round me and take my hand."

We pressed his cold hand. Someone asked:

"Jerry, do you know you are dying?"

"Oh, yes! I realize that."

"Are you afraid to die?"

"Oh, no! I am perfectly happy. I have discharged my duty to my country—'dulce est pro patria mori.' "

He closed his eyes, and we thought for the last time. Rousing up again, he said:

"How dark it grows. Come nearer, boys. I can't see you, but take my hand, each one of you, so I can feel that

123

you are all near me. Boys, I want you to promise me one thing."

"What is it, Jerry?"

"I want you to bury me. Will you promise to bury me?"

"Yes, Jerry, we will bury you, and put you in a neat coffin."

"No, not that. You can't bury all in coffins, and I want to be buried like my comrades. But deep, boys, deep, so the beasts won't get me."

He was evidently thinking of the Federal graves we passed on the battlefield of Chancellorsville. We promised—there was a gasp, a quiver of the form, and Jerry Gage, the southern patriot soldier fell asleep.[6]

*"Dulce est pro patria mori!"*

The cannonading had ceased, and quiet reigned over the hills around Gettysburg, the ominous calm before the storm. Soon the "Rebel Yell" announced that the charge was in progress, and soon the wounded began to come in a continuous stream. It was late at night before we sent off our wounded, and we were too tired to walk back to the division hospital, although we were very hungry, and that was the only chance for something to eat, so each man got him an armful of hay, made him a bed and was soon fast asleep. About midnight, or later, one of my men awakened me, whispering:

"Ain't you hungry? Come with me, we have something to eat."

Although it looked a little selfish not to invite the others, I went with my man to a farm house nearby, where I found my litter corps sitting around a nicely roasted pig.

"Come, Doctor, we haven't much bread, and no salt, but I think we can eat this pig, and enjoy it."

And we did enjoy it. Early morning found me back at the hospital, where we were busy all day, performing necessary operations, and re-dressing the wounds of the first day's fight. On the morning of the 6th, Surgeon Hubbard summoned me to his tent.

"Wilson," he said, "the army is going to move tomorrow, and I will detail you to remain here with the wounded."

The announcement stunned me, and I could not speak for a moment. At last I said:

"Doctor, I will obey orders, but if you have any duty more dangerous or more arduous, let me have it. I don't want to fall into the hands of the enemy, although I know they will treat me right. I am real cranky on this subject. Please give me something else."

"Well," said he, "you have had a hard time, and I wanted to do you a favor. I have a train of wounded to start to Williamsport. Can you be ready in half an hour?"

"I am ready now, just as soon as I can get my blankets and pocket case of instruments, bandages and a bottle of morphine, and I thank you to boot. Where is the train?"

"Out on the pike."

I inspected my train, examining each wagon and ambulance, to see the character of cases I had, and filling a haversack with bandages and such things as I thought I might need, and started.

This wagon train was simply immense and was said to be thirty miles long when closed up. My portion of the train was in the latter half of it, and we started for Wil-

liamsport, Md., about 11 o'clock, distance about fifty
miles.[7] It was very warm, and the wounded men were considerably crowded in some of the wagons which made it
very disagreeable. About one o'clock we had a very hard
rain which was gratefully received by the soldiers. It
cooled them off and added much to their comfort. We
traveled all day, all night, all the next day and I reached
Williamsport about ten o'clock at night. When near
Hagerstown a squadron of Federal cavalry darted in at a
cross-road and captured all my section of the train, except-
ing about twenty-five ambulances that had passed the
cross-road. I saw the Yankees when they struck the train
and I ran back and ordered the slightly wounded men
who were walking along with the train to climb over the
fence and get into the woods, which they did, and I guess
more than a hundred saved themselves from capture. The
Yankees remained but a short while and went off after the
captured wagons, and the train moved on.[8]

When I reached Williamsport I found the streets all
barricaded with wagons, and I thought I would never get
into the town. Had it been light I would have had no
trouble, but I had to feel my way, and finally crawled
over two or three wagons and reached an open street
which I followed until I found a house with lights and
heard a female voice singing.

When I reached the house I found a lady sitting on
the portico enjoying the night breeze, for the weather was
very warm. I walked up on the portico and speaking
politely, asked if I could get shelter for the night.

The light from the window showed plainly that I was
a Confederate officer.

"Are you sick or wounded?" she asked.

"Neither, madam. I am a surgeon, and was sent back with the wounded, and have been trying to get into the town through this wilderness of wagons for an hour; can you tell me what it all means?"

"Oh, yes! The Federal cavalry threatened the town and Gen. [John D.] Imboden[9] had only a small force so he barricaded all the street with wagons but one, then he armed the teamsters and they are all out tonight guarding Gen. Lee's trains and the town. But excuse me sir, have you been to supper?"

"No, ma'am, I have not tasted food in thirty hours. I started with rations but I gave them to the wounded soldiers."

"Well have a seat and I will have your supper ready in a few minutes."

I was thinking pretty rapidly. This is the first friendly woman I have seen since I crossed the Potomac into Maryland. I am certainly lucky, and I never wanted to find one any worse. I will just wait and see if she is southern or—

"Walk in to supper, Doctor," she said pleasantly, and familiarly, putting an end to my thoughts, and the Doctor obeyed orders like a good soldier.

"Will you have tea, or coffee, Doctor?"

"Coffee, if you please, ma'am."

"It is hardly worthwhile to ask a soldier that question," she said. "You soldiers all seem fond of coffee."

"Yes, ma'am. I guess we need a nervous stimulant, and it is certainly a very fine one, and very palatable."

She handed my coffee, helped my plate bountifully, and sat down on the opposite side. For a few moments not a word was spoken, and I was eating ravenously.

"Madam," said I, "will you grant me a favor?"

"Certainly, Doctor. What is it?"

"Keep on talking. It has been so long since I heard a lady's voice, it sounds like sweet music to my ears, and I am really ashamed for you to watch me eat, I am so mortal hungry."

Breaking into a merry laugh, she said: "Eat right along, Doctor. I won't watch you, and don't take time to grow sentimental."

"Sentimental! If your kindness, splendid supper and voice did not stir up a little sentiment in the heart of a Confederate soldier, who is a thousand miles from wife, sisters, home, and among his enemies, I would write him heartless, and think he ought to be court martialed and shot."

"You are among friends tonight," she quickly said, in a lower voice, and rose, and walking to the door of the kitchen, closed it, as if she was afraid someone would hear us talking. I was satisfied, and felt happy and thankful. She returned and talked on pleasantly, until my Confederate stomach was full—satisfied. After some sweet music on the piano by my hostess, she said:

"I see you are very tired, Doctor. Take this candle and go into that room and go to bed, and I hope you will get a good night's rest."

Thanking her, I walked into the room and closed the door. I noticed the windows were up. When I looked at the bed with its snow-white covering, I was afraid to get upon it, but I determined to dirty it as little as possible, so I undressed for the first time since the 13th day of June, and went to bed like a christian. The sun was shining brightly when I awoke the next morning. I guess I would have slept all day long, if I had not been forcibly awakened. After breakfast, I inquired the way to Gen. Imboden's headquarters. The lady came out on the portico to show me. Handing her a $5 Confederate bill, I said:

"Madam, let me pay you for my night's enjoyment and comfort. I am sorry I have nothing better than my country's poor currency to pay you with."

"No, sir, I won't have a cent. Come and stay with me as long as you remain in Williamsport."

Said I: "Take it and keep it, as a souvenir of the war."

"No, Doctor, I won't have a cent, and it will do you some good."

"Well, I expect I will have to go right on to Winchester, and we will never meet again. Good by! Thanks for your kindness. And may God bless you and yours."

A tear dimmed the little woman's eye. "Another green spot in the soldier's path." I hurried on to the General's headquarters, thinking of the pleasant incident, thinking of the dear little woman, and wondering if I could manage to see her again. I found Gen. Imboden[10] to be a fine looking, jolly old gentleman of about fifty years, quick in his manner, and looked straight at you when talking, wasting no words.

"Go down to the river, and get the wounded across as rapidly as possible, Doctor. You will find it slow and hard work, as I have but one ferryboat. There are 50 extra ambulances on the other side, and surgeons to accompany them to the hospitals at Jordan Springs and Winchester. When you get them across, report to me."

I found it rather slow work, but kept the boat running regularly, and about 3 p.m. saw my last load start over, and I turned my steps toward headquarters to report the fact to the General. The General thanked me, and seemed gratified to know that the wounded were all safely across the river, and on the way to the hospital, where their wounds could be dressed. Poor fellows! They were suffering, and the General knew it. One care at least, was off his mind.

Gen. Imboden asked me where I was ordered to report. I answered:

"To the Chief Surgeon at Winchester."

"Hurry up," he said, "for the ambulances may leave you. I think you will find them on top of the hill where they camped last night."

I saluted and turned to go. The old man extended his hand and said:

"Good bye! I am very much obliged to you."

I hurried away, and when I reached the top of the hill beyond the river, the ambulances were all gone, and I was considerably perplexed. I was thirty miles from Winchester. The sun was little more than an hour high, and I knew nothing of the road, and the trip must be made in the night. I must think about it. I found a seat near the roadside, where I could watch the ferry and the road. I concluded to go on if an opportunity offered, that is, if anyone came across going in the direction of Winchester. If not, I will go back and spend the night with my good friend, and make the trip in daylight. I felt very much inclined to do this, and I think I had decided.

Suddenly a cannon shot across the river, shook the earth, and reverberated among the hills. Another, and still another, and then the musketry began to rattle and I knew a fight was in progress. The enemy was attacking

Williamsport.[11] The ferry was across the river. I hastened up the hill hoping I might get a view of the fight, and was just in time to see the enemy charge Gen. Imboden's forces. The battle lasted but a short while, and the attack was handsomely repulsed; and the "Rebel Yell" announced the fact that the wagoners were in turn charging the enemy. By this time the smoke over the battlefield obscured everything, friends and foe alike, and I returned to my post, determined to go back to Williamsport and spend the night with my friend, and learn the results of the "Wagoners Battle." As I looked towards the ferry I saw a vehicle drawn by two fine looking horses starting up the steep hill. As it drew near, a familiar voice cried out:

"Hello, Wilson, what in the d——l are you doing here?"

I would have known that voice among a thousand; Capt. B. F. Jones, our old Commissary.[12]

"I might ask the same question, Captain, with propriety, but I will ask you, where are you going?"

"To Winchester, but get in Doctor, my horses can't stand here on this steep hillside, and we can talk as we ride along."

"Well, Captain, you always turn up at the right time and place," I said as I crawled into the surry.

"I am exceedingly glad to see you, but why you found me just where you did will require some time to explain. Are you directly from the army?"

"Yes, I left it about noon, and drove on to Williamsport, and hearing the Yankees attack the place, I thought I had better be on the safe side, so I drove on across the Potomac, and will go to Winchester tonight, as my horses are fresh and need exercise."

After asking after my friends, I gave my own history, in a few words, and we rode on talking of the army and the friends we had lost at Gettysburg. Captain Jones was the first one of my regiment that I had a chance to talk to, and it was really a relief to me, although he brought sad tidings in regard to many of my particular friends.

"Wilson, let us drive up to the first farm house and get something to eat for my horses and ourselves, and by that time the moon will be up."

"All right, Captain, you are the Commissary, if you will find the grub, I will help you eat it, as I have always done."

The moon rose while we were eating and resting and we had a pleasant, but all night's, drive, to Winchester.

"Where did you get your nice rig, Captain?"

"I got it near Gettysburg, from an old Dutch farmer."

"Buy it?"

"Not much. I borrowed it."

"Weren't you afraid to do such a thing after Gen. Lee's strict orders in regard to appropriating private property?"

"Yes, I was, but I thought catching came before hanging and I was ordered to report at once to the Secretary of War, at Richmond, and I could get across the Potomac before the old fellow could report me, and by the little transaction save walking about 150 miles, and you know I never could walk, it makes my feet sore."

"Well, those were great temptations, but, honestly, did not your conscience hurt you when you took those fine horses from the old man?"

"Yes, it did, but I happened to think of their d—m soldiers taking the last pound of meat and flour on my place in Mississippi last spring, and leaving my wife and children without a thing to eat, and my old Confederate heart turned to stone."

"But I am glad Gen. Lee issued those strict orders, and I believe that they have been generally obeyed, for I want the Yankee nation and the whole world to see the difference between their leaders and ours, or between their soldiers and ours."

And thus we talked as we rode on toward Winchester.

As the sun rose, we rode into the old town, and putting up the horses, went to a hotel and went to bed, asking the landlord to wake us at noon. We were promptly called at 12 m. We dined together for the last time, bade each other good by, Capt. Jones going on to Richmond, I to look up the post surgeon, and report for duty.

I was placed in charge of a large new church, which was being used as a hospital. Here I went into the wholesale receiving and forwarding business.[13] For three long weeks I suppose I dressed the wounds of from thirty to fifty men every day, and shipped them on up the valley to Staunton. Many of these wounds had not been dressed since the battle, and were in a terrible condition. I don't know how the poor fellows stood it, but I never heard a murmur. Their wounds were very offensive, and 90 per cent were infested with vermin. It would frequently require a half an hour or longer to get the maggots out of a wound, and when you remember that we had no disinfectants, you can understand why it was so tedious, why it was so disagreeable.[14] It was certainly the most disagreeable duty I ever performed. I was engaged at it from morning till night, taking time at noon to go to dinner. In a few days I began to lose my appetite, simply because

133

I could never remove the offensive odor from my hands, and of course I began to lose flesh. In a short time I began to have fever. I could see no place to stop and rest. The poor men must be attended to, and there was no one else, it seemed, to do the work. I asked the Post Surgeon for an assistant, but no assistant was sent me, and if it had not been for the good ladies of Winchester, who came to the rescue, and helped me in every way possible, I don't know what I would have done. They made and brought me bandages, soft cloths, soap and everything they could furnish, and one dear old mother brought me every morning a bucketful of a strong decoction of elder, which helped me very much in getting rid of the vermin. To say nothing of the good edibles and rich soups furnished the poor fellows.

Certainly the women of Winchester were ministering angels to our wounded soldiers.

In the midst of dinner, one day, a band on the street struck up "Dixie."

"What in the world does that mean?" said "mine host," leaving the table and room.

In a short time he returned and in a sad tone reported that the army was falling back, and was marching through the town.

"And that means," said he "that we will be again left in the hands of our enemies."

Poor old man, I was sorry for him, sorry that such a person should have to be left to the tender mercies of the foe.

I rose from the table and reached the street in time to find a portion of my division passing. Dr. Hubbard came along in his ambulance and saw me.

"Hello, Wilson, what are you doing here?"

"I have just finished my dinner, and am waiting to see what troops are passing."

"Are you sick?"

"I hope not, Doctor."

"Why man, you have a hot fever," he said, taking my hand, "and you look like a ghost. What have you been doing?"

I gave him my history for three weeks.

"Well, get into this ambulance, you shall not go back to that hospital again. I have made two requisitions for you, and they were disregarded. So get in and I will take you along with me."

I returned to the house to pay my board, and to bid the old people goodbye. Not a cent would they have for my board.

"Can't do too much for the Confederate soldier," seemed to be the sentiment and motto of the people. Glorious people! No wonder the enemy could never hold the town when attacked by the Confederates. It was a boon to fight for such a people. And they were only a sample of the South.

Gen. Lee fell back leisurely across the mountains to a position south of the Rapidan, where we enjoyed a season of rest and the luxury of a bath, clean clothes and freedom from graybacks.

I enjoyed my ride in Dr. Hubbard's ambulance across the mountain and especially did I enjoy the peculiar medicine the Doctor carried in a big black bottle, stowed away in his ambulance. It proved to be a most excellent appetizer, and for want of a better name, I dubbed it Hubbard's Tonic.

135

When I saw my regiment on dress parade for the first time after our return to Virginia, the change the short campaign had made caused a pang of sorrow. The regiment was in command of a Captain. The Colonel, dead, the Lieutenant-Colonel, a hopeless cripple and the Major severely wounded. Our gallant Adjutant escaped. Many of the company officers gone and in the ranks, great gaps, great gaps![15]

But as I wish to emphasize the pleasant memories of the war I will refrain from calling up its bitter sorrows.

## XXI

## *The Scout*

---◄◆►---

There was a class of men in the army that always interested one very much, and whose history and adventures if written up, would prove intensely interesting. I allude to the scouts.

There was a little boy, I suppose 14 years old, but unusually small of stature, if he was so old, who was often seen riding with the generals. He seemed to be under no discipline, and went where and when he pleased. He was called Gen. Lee's spy, and was said to visit Washington, Baltimore, or any point in the Federal lines desired. Much said of this boy may have been untrue or exaggerated, but there were scouts that performed gallant and daring deeds, and were of great value to their commanders in gaining information in regard to the enemy, and learning their numbers, position, etc.

Gen. Heth had a noted scout who was called John. I knew him, and met him often. He was a peculiar man, always by himself, talking very little, and seemed to be always thinking. John would never talk of his exploits, and he did not permit those who accompanied him to talk.

One evening I walked down to the Rapidan, ostensibly to bathe. I found John lying behind a log gazing over the country beyond the river through a large field glass or telescope. He was looking more particularly in the direction of the Bubbies, two beautifully formed twin mountains, which received their names from their marked resemblance to that interesting and important portion of the female anatomy.

"John, what are you looking at?"

"Do you see those tents over yonder on the Bubbies?"

"No, I can see nothing resembling a tent."

"Look to the left of the nearest mountain. Don't you see them?"

"I believe I see two white spots about the size of a newspaper, but they certainly are not tents."

"Come and look through this glass, Doctor."

I looked, and was astonished. It drew those Yankees so close I could almost count the buttons on their uniforms and hear them talk.

"How far are those mountains, John?"

"About 12 miles. See if you can count the men, Doctor? That is what I have been trying to do for an hour."

I did my best. "John, I believe there are twelve!"

"You are pretty good for the first trial, but there are fifteen, and I think twenty."

"Are you going for them tonight, John?"

"I don't know. I will watch them and decide. You can look out for their tents in the morning."

This was more than I ever got out of John before, and I became very much interested, and determined to watch. Late in the evening John passed my tent quietly, almost stealthily, going toward the ford, two men following him, all seemed to be armed alike, a Sharp's 5 shot rifle, and a heavy army pistol, Colt's six-shooter. I followed them at a distance, and saw them cross the river in a little boat, and strike out toward the mountains in single file, John in front. I could not sleep well that night, for thinking of those three daring men.

Next morning I rose early and went out to look for those tents. They were not to be seen. An hour or so later three jaded men rode quietly into camp, each leading a horse with the carbine and holsters of a Federal trooper attached to the saddle. What had they done? They would never tell.

# XXII

## Home on Furlough

One morning toward the last of August, Dr. Hubbard came into my tent, and after asking after my health, and the health of the regiment, said:

"You are not looking well, Wilson, and I think you had better go home for a while. Send up your application, and I will put an endorsement on it that will carry it through. I think you deserve a furlough."

This was a compliment I was not expecting and a kindness I could never forget. The application was sent up and returned approved, and in three days I started home with pockets filled with letters to the homefolks from the boys of Co. D.[1] I boarded the train Sept. 1st, for Richmond where we could get transportation to the nearest point to our homes in North Mississippi. Our homes were within the Federal lines. I found four boys going to the same part of the State, and we determined to have a good time, and buy everything we saw, good to eat or drink on the road. By doing this we had plenty and good grub at that. If we had depended on eating at hotels we would have starved to death almost. Sometimes we would buy a stack of pies and things, then a bucket of boiled eggs and a basket of sandwiches and every now and then a bottle of pine top, and so we went toward home. We got transportation to Okolona, Miss., on the M. & O. R. R. which was 125 miles south of the Confederate outpost on the Tallahatchie river. This gap we traversed in a hack which cost us 150 Confederate dollars.[2]

We drove that hack for all it was worth. Left Okolona at sunset and slept upon the side walk in Pontotoc 27 miles distant. Starting early next morning, we made 55 miles and would have gone further but our horses were failing. Starting at daylight we made it to the Tallahatchie river by 1 p.m., paid our hack driver, who swore he would never drive soldiers again. We bathed in the river and dressed up to meet our friends and loved ones. Three of us, who were going to Chulahoma, found horses to ride, the other two struck off on foot, and I suppose we all reached home before dark.[3]

We were warned by the cavalry picket to look out for the enemy, but we felt like we were at home and looking out for friends and not our enemies; still we felt weary and did not enjoy our visit like we would have done, had we been within the Confederate lines. Friends came in to get letters from their boys in the army, and they told us to feel easy, that they would warn us if a cavalry raid was sent out from Memphis.[4]

We found our country had been pretty well stripped by the enemy, and many people were living pretty hard, but we heard no grumbling, found the people as true as steel and hopeful of results.

We started back to Virginia on Oct. 1st. We were four days making the trip back to Okolona, then six to Richmond.[5]

The next day by noon we reached Gordonsville and found the army had gone north toward Washington City. Here we were stopped, and all returning soldiers were armed and put into the lines around the place to defend the stores and the railroad communications south and west.

Fortunately no raids were sent against us, and we only had to wait for orders to go forward and join commands. Here we remained anxiously awaiting orders for two long weary weeks. This was a trait of character peculiar to the Confederate soldier that shone out most brilliantly. If he was not at home with the loved ones, he wanted to be in camp with the boys, sharing their joys, sorrows and privations.

At last orders came and a considerable body of men, several thousand in number, moved forward across the Rapidan and Culpeper county to join their commands on the Rappahannock. Here we remained, fortunately for us, but a short while. Winter was rapidly approaching, the nights were becoming fearfully cold, we were needing our winter clothing and extra blankets which were far in the rear to shield us against the blasts of an early winter.

We were told when we reached camp, that Gen. Lee had been for days inviting and waiting for an attack from the enemy, who occupied the country south of the Rappahannock, desirous to strike one more blow before going into winter quarters.

A few nights after joining our commands, about 3 o'clock, we were aroused from our slumbers, as we sat around our camp-fires nodding, trying to sleep, and at the same time keep from freezing. We fell into line with exceeding great joy, believing we were going to make the last tramp of the season.

We were marched back two or three miles, and about daylight we were drawn up in line of battle in an open field facing the north, where the cold northwest wind chilled us to the marrow. Here we waited all day for the enemy to attack us. In the evening there was some artillery firing, and skirmishing on our extreme left, but the gage of battle was declined, and as the sun went down we wheeled into line and started south at quick time.[6]

After passing Culpeper Court House we came to fires built all along the pike, where we could warm ourselves. These fires had been built by the pioneer corps, which had been sent on ahead for that purpose.

It was bitterly cold, and the ground was frozen as hard as iron, and a brisk wind was blowing from the north, but we protected ourselves against the wind with our blankets, and no one was injured or frozen.

The beautiful twin mountains, the Bubbies, had camp fires all around them, and over them, as if the army had gone into camp. These fires had been built by the Cavalry, and kept burning, to deceive the enemy, and enable Gen. Lee to remove everything south of the Rapidan. They looked beautiful indeed, and very enticing to cold soldiers. We marched all night without halting to rest, and about 9 o'clock we crossed the Rapidan on improvised bridges, and ascended the hills beyond, the men cheering as lustily as they did five months before, when crossing the Potomac into Maryland.

The army was soon in the positions desired by our Generals, and went to work with a will to protect themselves against the inclemency of the weather.

Winter quarters were always hailed by the soldiers with joy and delight. First, because it brought a period of rest and comparative comfort after the arduous trials and struggles of the summer campaign.

Then, too, it was the season to get furloughs home, and write home letters giving an account of our trials, joys and sorrows to the loved ones there. A time for reflection and thankfulness.

But we must first build the huts, and make them comfortable. These were built this season of pine logs split open, and just as long and wide as the tent to go over them. The pen is built with chimney and door in the front end of the hut. This plan gave us more room than any other we could devise. The bed was like a big box, and was filled with clean pine straw in lieu of feathers.

The pen and chimney is now carefully daubed with mud, the tent is carefully stretched over the pen, the fly over the tent, and now the back, jambs and hearth complete the soldiers' winter quarters, and it is a very comfortable house, and soon becomes home to the soldier.[7]

# XXIII

## Chaplain Witherspoon

————◆▶————

This chapter is devoted entirely to our noble Chaplain and his work. The one great man in his brigade. The perfect christian gentleman, if such a term can ever be applied to frail humanity.

Rev. Thos. Dwight Witherspoon[1] was appointed Chaplain of Davis' Brigade, in June 1863. Up to this time he had been Chaplain of the 12th Miss., in which regiment he enlisted in the early days of the war, giving up his important work and church in the city of Oxford, Miss., to cast in his lot with his country's soldiers, and preach to them the glorious gospel of the Son of God. I heard him preach his first sermon in the brigade, on the lines in front of Fredericksburg, just before we started on the long march to Gettysburg, and next on the Sabbath before the battle of Gettysburg, as already stated.

After returning to Virginia, during the rest given the army in August and September, he held services regularly and a great revival commenced in the brigade, which lasted to the end of the struggle.[2] This revival was general throughout the army, east and west, but I confine my account of it to my own brigade.

At Gettysburg, Chaplain Witherspoon went into the battle at the head of his regiment and fought through it with his company, and escaped the bullets of the enemy. After that he was requested by men and officers not to

145

risk his valuable life again, but to repair to the hospital and give his sole attention to the wounded. Here on the field with the wounded and suffering soldiers, our love and friendship had its birth, which has lived and grown stronger as the years have passed, and will blossom in eternity.

I can testify to his efficiency and untiring energy in his ministrations to the wounded, in both temporal and spiritual things. Chaplain Witherspoon endeared himself to every man in brigade by his kindly disposition and genial manner. He was every man's friend, and the oldest and youngest soldier felt no hesitation in approaching him in time of trouble. He was physically a delicate man, but intellectually a giant. He was a devout, humble, hopeful christian, and his daily walk and example was a benediction to his brigade.

He was a faithful, earnest, simple preacher of the gospel, and the youngest and most illiterate soldier could understand his deepest, grandest sermons. His labors were incessant and abundant, and during winter quarters he taught two or three classes in the languages and mathematics. He had a fine library, which was free, and a great boon to the soldiers during the winter's rest.

When we commenced building our huts for the winter Chaplain Witherspoon called for volunteers to build a chapel. Although it was bitterly cold, and everyone was anxious to get under shelter, fifty men offered themselves, and with these he went into the pine forest, and by the time we completed our huts, they had up the walls of a spacious building, 30 x 40 feet, two large fireplaces and chimneys, and ready for the roof. New workmen came forward and we soon had our chapel covered, daubed, seated and ready for services. The first Sabbath after completion it was dedicated. Dr. [B. F.] Lacy, Gen. Jackson's old chaplain, preached the sermon, which was listened to by as many as could pack into that house, while many, very many, climbed onto the roof, and slipping aside a board so they could both see and hear, listened attentively and reverently to the man of God.

Text—Exodus, 20th chapter, and latter part of 24th verse: "In all places where I record my name I will come unto thee, and I will bless thee."

The whole service was most appropriate and impressive, and the sermon a masterpiece in itself. The closing sentences are still remembered:

"My young friends," said the venerable man of God, "I am told that many of you have recently enlisted under the banner of the Cross. That many of you have started out on the Christian warpath. You will need all the encouragement and comfort you can get. You can get all the encouragement and comfort you need in God's blessed word. Read it carefully, study it prayerfully, asking the Holy Spirit to guide and direct you, and don't forget your prayers. And if you feel embarrassed in kneeling down to pray before your comrades, come here to this chapel, where God has not only promised to meet with you, but to bless you, and pour out your souls to God."

All through that long, dreary winter I visited that chapel at different hours of the day, and I never found it empty, someone always praying, and toward the close of the day, at the twilight hour, on raising the curtain and entering the sanctuary, you would find from ten to twenty silent worshippers kneeling in different parts of the chapel in silent prayer, not a word nor a whisper, only now and then a sob.

Truly God was in that place, and it was the very gate of Heaven to our souls.

Here we had services morning and evening on the Sabbath, and prayer-meeting Wednesday night. Here the Christian Association of the brigade met once a month, enrolled the names of all new converts, and those names, with appropriate letters, sent to the churches at home, and sweet letters from the home churches, read and wept over.

## *Winter Diversions*

———◆▶———

The boys had nothing, in camp, during winter quarters to amuse themselves and counteract nostalgia, the bane of military inactivity, but the various games played by soldiers, such as cards, checkers, dominoes and chess.[1] And many expert players were developed in all these games. The writer remembers many a pleasant hour spent over the fascinating chess board with his dear old comrade, Lt. Anthony, of the 11th Miss. regiment, who was the first chess player in the Army of Northern Virginia.

Other amusements were devised by the men but none were more enjoyed or far reaching in value than the Glee Club, or Minstrel Club organized by the members of the brigade band. All had stringed instruments, Bass Viol, Bones,[2] Violins, Tamborines and Banjos, and all were blessed with magnificent voices, and after practicing awhile they rendered music that would astonish the natives and would have been pronounced first class in any of our cities. I have heard the Campbell and Chrystie Minstrels in the good old days before "the unpleasantness" but I never heard any music, or singing that surpassed this band in sweetness and pathos.

When they would render "Old Folks at Home," or "I'm Going Back to Dixie," or "Sweet Evalina," it would be followed by a cheer that would cause your hair to straighten out.

When Sweeny, Gen. Stuart's celebrated banjoist, walked upon the stage and, sweeping his magic hand over his wonderful instrument, struck up "Old Bob Ridley," and the whole Ridley family would come on the stage one at a time, as they were called by the musician, and join in the reel; the female portion dressed in the most grotesque costumes, and all as black as Sambo in his palmiest days, you would begin to laugh, and laugh until your sides would ache.

This band was worth more to the brigade as a "health promoter" than the two Surgeons would have been with well filled chests of medicine.

## *Mine Run Fizzle*

Early one morning, about Dec. 1st, we were ordered to be in line in one hour in light marching order, which meant that particular morning, one blanket and an empty haversack.

During the active campaign such an order would have been hailed with delight, but to be rustled out of our snug quarters in mid winter and start on the war path in light marching order, was a very different thing. It meant hardship, it meant suffering.

Hastily cooking and swallowing our breakfast we were ready, and the command being given, we started at quick time for the "plank road." This plank road ran due east and west through Orange county to Fricksburg. The reader must remember this to understand what follows.

When we reached the plank road we started east. The reader must also remember that the position of our army was due north of the Confederate Capital, which was the bone of contention and the object of the enemy.

"On to Richmond!"

Everything and everybody was in a rush, artillery, ordnance wagons and ambulances were pressing to the front. Every now and then the troops would be ordered out of the road for a battery to pass, and then would be put at a double quick to regain what we had lost. Before we had gone three miles pretty heavy firing commenced some distance (10 or 12 miles) ahead and to the right (south) of the road we were traveling.

This firing of artillery and musketry gradually increased and was extending south, or to our right, very rapidly. We continued to press forward. You could hear but one command:

"Close up, men, and press forward!"

We were marching through a heavily wooded country and frequently had to get off the plank road. And the officers and men were so eager to get on they would try it through the woods as the artillery and wagons were passing.

In the general melee I became separated from my command, but I kept right on down the road after them. We seemed to be getting nearer the battle which was raging almost directly north of us now, and was bearing in the direction of Richmond.

After going two or three miles farther I came to an open field on the left, or north side, of the road, where I found two wagons standing and a couple of tents. Here I also found a staff officer sitting on his horse and directing the line to turn directly to the right into the woods, stack arms and rest.

It was a strange looking procedure and I was puzzled to know what it meant. The battle had passed us, or we had passed it, and was still raging. I walked out towards the tents, and found it was Gen. Lee's Headquarters. Col. [Walter H.] Taylor, Adj. General, was sitting on a box busily writing and seemingly unconscious of the fight going on out yonder, directly between our army and Richmond.

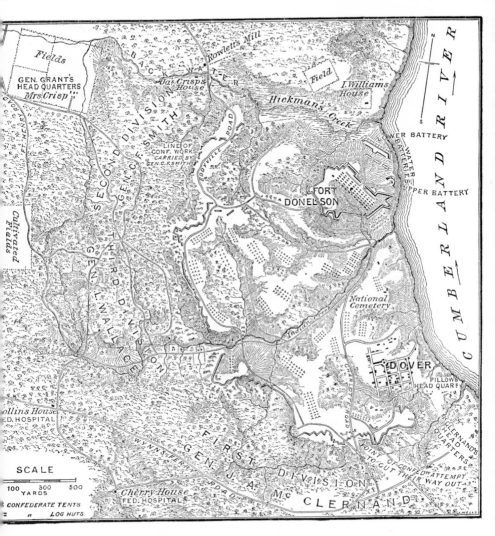

MAP OF FORT DONELSON

BETWEEN THE LINES DURING A TRUCE

LLECTING THE WOUNDED

CHARLES CLARK
Governor of Mississippi
1863–65

THE HOLLOW SQU

REVEREND
T. D. WITHERSPOON

HE CIVIL WAR

THE TOWN OF DOVER FROM ROBINSON HILL

DEPOT AND TISHOMINGO HOTEL

THE GUNBOAT CONESTOGA

"GOOD-BYE"

Presently Gen. Lee rode up with two or three atten-
dants, and dismounting, gave Traveler to an orderly, and
walking to an old pine tree, called for his guide.

An old man with white hair, in the garb of a citizen,
walked out of the tent and approached the General, who
drew a map out of his pocket, and asked this old gentleman several questions in regard to it. I was not quite near
enough to hear what was said, but I imagined Gen. Lee
looked anxious and troubled. The battle was progressing
and now directly between us and the Capital.

General Lee asked:

"Where is Gen. Stuart?"

"I don't know, General," answered Col. Taylor, "but
I see Gen. [John B.] Gordon riding up, he can probably
tell you."

Gen. Gordon dismounted, going to the pine tree. The
Generals talked earnestly together for a few moments.
Gordon saluted, sprang upon his fine horse and went off
in a gallop toward the battlefield. Gen. Lee dictated two
orders, which were sent off, and then leaning against the
old pine tree, seemed to be earnestly thinking. I was thinking also and growing more uneasy. I was rapidly losing
my faith.

Has Gen. Lee been caught napping at last? Has Gen.
Meade succeeded in flanking us on the right while we have
been enjoying our comfortable huts and has a formidable
force between our army and Richmond, that can and will
destroy our depot of stores and supplies at Gordonsville,
tear up our railroad communications and force us, if nothing worse, to fall back into the defenses of Richmond?

Such thoughts rapidly passed through my brain. My

anxiety was intense, my faith was rapidly growing thread-bare. I stood looking at Gen. Lee, who was leaning quietly against that old pine tree seemingly lost in thought. The battle was still raging out yonder toward the Capital and getting farther south. The troops were still pressing up from the west, and came laughing and cheering as they rapidly marched down the plank road.

Gen. Lee turned and spoke to Col. Taylor, who instantly called out:

"Bill! oh, Bill!"

"Sir," came from one of the tents.

"Bring that roll of blankets here, Gen. Lee wants to take a nap."

Bill brought out a large roll of blankets and unrolled them at the foot of that pine tree and the old hero stretched himself upon his pallet, with his "spurs on." Bill covered him up carefully, and he soon seemed to be quietly sleeping. What a change! My cap went up into the air. My faith was suddenly restored. I could scarcely restrain the Rebel Yell. I uttered a silent reverent, thank God. Our stores and scanty stock of provisions at Gordonsville were safe, Richmond was safe and all was well.

Thus ended "Meade's Fizzle," as the soldiers dubbed it, the best conceived plan yet devised by Federal Generals to reach the Confederate Capital had been signally thwarted, and their Generals and Cavalry taught that Gen. Lee's rear was a dangerous place to find.[1]

We bivouacked in the woods that night, and the next day marched back to our winter quarters. Returning by country roads, giving up the plank road to the Artillery and wagons, that all might get back to camp sooner and more comfortably.

Our command moved south to strike a parallel road, which carried us through a considerable portion of the battlefield of the day before, won by Stuart's troopers, over a largely superior force of the enemy's "picked" cavalry.

For more than ten miles we passed dead horses, broken caissons, a piece or two of abandoned artillery, with here and there those little hillocks, showing where brave men had fought and perished. We reached our comfortable quarters late in the evening, and they never looked more comfortable. We had marched about thirty-five miles on light rations, and were hungry and weary.

# XXVI

## A Practical Joke

---

"Hello! Wilson, what are you doing?"

This question was asked by my messmate, Capt. John Powell.[1]

"I am writing, or have just finished a letter to my wife, Captain. I have a chance to send a letter by hand, the only way she can get one now, as she is within the Federal lines, and they have no connection with the Southern mails, except as they find someone returning who will bring the letters through and mail them at some point in Dixie. I thought I would write her a Christmas and birthday letter, as both occur on the same day."

"And this is Christmas eve, is it? How I wish I could be at home one short week, with the girls and the old folks! How I would enjoy it, especially the good grub. Just think of the turkey, old ham, the nice cake and custard, besides the thousand other good things that will be consumed in old Grenada, tomorrow, and John Powell won't get a smell. I tell you, Doctor, I don't see how I am going to stand it."

"Well, Captain, don't take it so hard. I am afraid you are taking a severe attack of nostalgia. Permit me to see your tongue. Exactly! The symptoms are unmistakable, and you must visit the minstrels at once. Like Saul of old, an evil spirit has come upon you, and Sweeney must play his banjo."

156

"Oh, thunder! Quit your foolishness, Doctor, and sit down and let us have a common sense talk."

"All right, John Powell, go ahead."

"Well, I was going to tell you that I have been hungry for two months, and ———"

"Please tell me something I didn't know, John."

"And every night I dream of good dinners, and infairs, and wedding suppers I have enjoyed in the past before this 'unpleasantness' came upon us. Have you felt that way, Doctor?"

"I think I have, Captain. Had the same pleasant dreams to tantalize me, the same aching void our Commissary doesn't fill, and if you will not tell it in Gath, nor publish it on the streets of Askelon,[2] I will tell you confidentially that I have not had a belly full since I came back from my furlough in October."

"Well, Doctor, I would like very much to know why the rations have been reduced so much, and so suddenly. And if Gen. Lee knows it?"

"Yes, John Powell, you may rest assured that Gen. Lee knows it, and it is filling his great heart with sorrow, and I'd bet a ginger cake, if I had one, that his rations are reduced on the same scale."

"I don't believe it, Doctor. I don't believe that Old Virginia, or his thousands of friends all over the State, would suffer him to want for anything. They would send him everything he needs."

"I believe all that, Captain. But do you suppose, or think that Gen. Lee would enjoy such good things, or eat them, when he knew his soldiers were hungry, and suffering for food? No, sir, never! He is not that kind of a man."

"Well, Doctor, do you think there is serious danger of the enemy starving us out!"

"Not this winter, Captain. But what will next winter bring? I think we are just now entering upon the 'starvation period' of this horrid war. Everything points in that direction. The opening up of the Mississippi river by the Federals has cut us off from our beef fields in Texas, Louisiana and Arkansas. This is the reason we never see any beef now, and it is a great misfortune. Officers have been sent home to collect the 'tax in kind' imposed upon the farmers of the south by the Confederate States Congress for the support of the army. The farmers will pay that tax willingly, I have no doubt, and that will begin to come in pretty soon, and our condition will improve, but I am afraid the 'tax in kind' won't go far enough. I noticed the crops from Richmond to North Mississippi, when I went home three months ago, and as I came back, and I can tell you they were nothing extra, in fact I think they are far below an average. If crops are short, the tax will be short. There is another ugly thing staring us in the face, John, that is the effect the emancipation proclamation is going to have upon the negro as a laborer, as a producer. So far it seems to have had little effect on him. He has not realized that he is a free man. I have no fear of the negroes rising, mistreating or abusing our wives, children and old men. I had much rather risk mine among the negroes than with the Yankees, two to one. But when the negroes come to realize that they are free, they will become lazy and worthless, I am afraid, and prove a bad producer. Then where will our grub come from?"

"The prospect looks really gloomy, Doctor, as you

have presented the case. Now, what effect are these short rations going to have on the rank and file? Cause desertions?"

"I am afraid it will, if it lasts any length of time. I believe we have the best, the purest, the most patriotic army since the days of Valley Forge and Morristown, but continuous hunger, I am afraid, will neutralize or destroy patriotism. As long as we were fighting, it was all right. We know from experience that our men fight like demons when they are hungry, but here in camp, with little or nothing to do, no excitement, they can only sit and think of home and the good things there, and dream of good dinners, as we have been doing, I fear it will have a demoralizing effect that will decrease our numbers."

"Well, let's quit talking about it. It does no good, and can do none—"

"Hello! Is this the Surgeon's tent?" asked someone at the door."

"Yes, Come in."

"I have a note for Dr. Wilson and Capt. Powell."

"All right, I'm much obliged. Light our Confederate candle, Powell, and see what it is. We have been talking until it has grown dark. Here, read the note."
Special Order No. 1.

See that both of you are at my tent by 7:30 sharp. Bring your cups.     WARD & GREEN, Commanding.

"What in the world does it mean, Wilson?"

"It means, at least, that they have something good to drink, or they would not have commanded us to bring our cups, and I expect we will have something good to eat, also, and you may get full once more, Captain."

"Where do you suppose they got it?"

"Well, I believe I can tell you. I was around there about 10 o'clock, this morning, when a fine wagon and team drove in front of the tent, and we all went out to see what it meant, of course. An old gentleman crawled out of the wagon and grabbed Col. Green around the neck, and we had quite a hugging scene. When the gentlemen finished hugging, Col. Green introduced us to his brother from ——— county, Virginia. Now you very well know that a Virginia gentleman wouldn't come thirty miles to visit his brother in camp, Christmas Eve, and come in an empty wagon. Those big-hearted gentlemen are going to share their good things with their comrades and friends. Anything wrong in that, John Powell?"

"Nothing, Doctor. It is eminently right and proper, especially at this particular time."

"Well, what time is it, John?"

"It is 7 o'clock, sharp."

"Let's hurry up and be on time. Soldiers must be prompt."

When we reached the large hospital tent adjoining Ward and Green's private apartment, we found it lit up, and filled with soldiers of all grades, from Brigadier General down. All were talking and laughing more like school boys than soldiers. We pressed our way through the crowd, and paid our respects to our hosts. An improvised table in one corner of the tent was loaded down with good things. Some of the boys were roasting apples in the huge fire place, where a roaring fire was burning, that rendered the tent perfectly comfortable. Soon everything was in readiness, and the order rang out:

"Come up, gentlemen, and have your cups filled."

Sugar was put into the cup, then a steaming roasted apple and then the cup was filled from the black bottle or jug. This, we were told, was old Virginia apple-jack, and we soon became intimately acquainted with the old gentleman. Many toasts were proposed and drank such as, "Our Country," "The Army," "Our General," "The Old Folks at Home," "The Girl I Left Behind Me," etc. And many impromptu speeches made, some of them beautiful and appropriate, indeed apple-jack and Virginia cake were stirring up all the eloquence in our souls. Men were speaking who never attempted to speak before. Soon the lines became shaky, and some, at length, began to fall, but there was always a man to take the place of his fallen comrade. The gallant heroes were borne from the field, by loving hands, and tenderly laid away to rest. After while old fashioned egg-nog was substituted for apple-jack and after enjoying a cup or two of this old delicious Christmas drink, the entertainment closed and we wended our way to our several tents, at least those who were able to wend.

Christmas morning, the sun shining in my tent and roused me from my pleasures of the past night. John Powell was lying by me, snoring like an Irishman.

"Wake up, John Powell, wake up! Christmas gift," I said, nudging him in the commissary department.

"Well, what is it you want?"

"I want to ask you some serious questions. My conscience is hurting me. Were you at Green and Ward's party last night?"

"I was."

"Did you enjoy yourself?"

"I did, to my full capacity," a smile beginning to light up his countenance.

"Were you drunk, John?"

"No," said he, beginning to laugh, "why do you ask?"

"I will answer you by asking a few more questions. John Powell, was I drunk?"

"No."

"How did we get home?"

"Why, Doctor, we walked home."

"Well I am glad to know that our temperance record is still good. I was afraid I had fallen in that last action. I don't remember anything after Bob Ward's eloquent speech."

"Well, if I am any judge, we were both sober."

"Well, if I was certain you were a competent judge at the time my conscience would not hurt me, but probably we had better not investigate farther. But I wish I had a pint of that rich egg-nog this Christmas morning, and I am going down to my old company for I am satisfied if there are any eggs or whisky in ten miles of this camp Co. D. has got it, and I really need a smile."

I finished my toilet and walked out. Just then Frank King came out of his tent and started in my direction, but seeing me, stopped and beckoned to me.

"What is it, Frank?"

"Some of the boys," he said, in a whisper, "have got a little egg-nog, and we thought you would enjoy some Christmas morning, I was starting for you, when I saw you come out of your tent."

"All right. I told Powell if there was anything of the

162

kind in camp you boys would have it. Bully for Co. D!"

I drank egg-nog with the boys, and as I rose to go they invited me to come back at 1 p.m. to eat turkey with them.

"All right, boys," I said, "I'll be on hand."

When I reached my tent breakfast was waiting for me.

"What luck, Doctor?" said Powell, as I entered our tent.

"First class, Captain, the boys had a good egg-nog, but not quite so bountiful as Ward and Green's last night."

"Where in the world did they get the eggs and whisky?"

"I don't know, Captain, I didn't ask the boys because I thought it was contrary to army regulations to ask such questions at this particular time of the year. I simply drank my nog, asking no questions for conscience sake."

A few days later I sent a prescription to the hospital steward for whisky. The steward sent the prescription back with this indorsement:

"Jug dry, not a drop in it."

The scales fell from my eyes. I knew at once where the boys got their whisky. Co. D had played a practical joke upon their surgeon. This was really too good to keep but I determined that no one should know it.

# XXVII

## Preparing to Meet the Hosts of Grant

———————◄◆►———————

Christmas is over. We had a pretty good time, considering all things. The weather had been beautiful, bright, sunshiny days that were perfectly comfortable, and cool, moonshiny nights. We had flour issued to us, the first time in weeks, and we had the pleasure of enjoying the luxury of Confederate biscuits, along with the other good things.

The theatre had been the chief attraction during the week, and crowds attended the performance nightly. The minstrels had dramatized "Meade's Fizzle," and rendered it in fine style, to the delight and enjoyment of the boys, interspersing the scenes with the finest music.

The band played out the old year, and welcomed the new year with our own dear "Dixie," and this morning we start out on the historic year of 1864.

I might here turn aside and sum up the successes and reverses of the eventful year that has just been numbered with the past, but I have confined myself to the narration of scenes and incidents occurring immediately around me in my own command, and the Grand Army to which I belonged. I am not writing up a history of the war, but I do desire to write a history of the Confederate Soldier, and attempt to show him as he was on the march, in the camp, in the ditches, on the battlefield, and I shall endeavor to pursue this plan to this end.

I am writing for the benefit of my own children and the benefit of their sons and daughters. The Confederate soldier was the same wherever you found him, in the East or in the West, at Gettysburg or Chickamauga. He was fighting for a "principle," the right to be free, for home, for "Dixie." He was not fighting for the negro, for bounty, for pay or pension.

The month of January was remarkably mild and full of sunshine, and the men were required to drill one hour each day, for practice and for exercise. The health of the army was never better, in fact it was almost perfect. Toward the close of the month the weather suddenly changed and turned very cold, and it began to snow, and it soon looked like winter had just commenced.

One morning I was roused from my slumbers, by shouts of laughter without. Hastily slipping into my pants and shoes, I went to the door, and drawing the curtain aside, stuck out my head to see what was going on, when a snowball about the size of a pumpkin struck me squarely in the face, and caused me to make a rapid retreat. Goodness! how cold! But it was a good shot. I dressed as rapidly as possible, and hurried out to take a hand in the fun. I was perfectly satisfied by the time Ellick called me to breakfast, but the fun and excitement continued to spread and increase, until regiments, brigades, and even divisions were arrayed against each other, commanded by their regular officers, and it was said that Gen. Lee himself witnessed the strange and terrible contest from the back of Traveler, and I have no doubt the old hero smiled at thought of his brave soldiers having for once, a cool and bloodless battle.

The cold and dreary winter drags its weary length

along. February was horrible, and March had come in like a roaring lion. The furloughed men and the wounded were returning in spite of the weather and the ranks were filling up, and we began to prepare for the great struggle that was coming in the early spring.

A company of sharpshooters was organized for each brigade and these picked marksmen were furnished cartridges to practice at the target, and we daily had fine specimens of marksmanship, at a distance ranging from 600 to 1200 yards.

The sharpshooters of Davis' brigade were placed under the command of Capt. Walker,[1] a very gallant young officer, who was very proud of his men, and drilled them in skirmish tactics, and shooting in every conceivable position. These men did effective work in the approaching campaign and were always in the front, and I have no doubt were the cause of the death of many a Federal officer. The men were being drilled any day the weather would permit, and were drilled at double-quick most of the time.

Mutterings of the coming storm were heard occasionally from beyond the Rappahannock and papers smuggled through the lines, announced the fact that "the hero of the West," Gen. U. S. Grant—the man of iron will—had been made Lieutenant-General. He was now perfecting his plans, concentrating his forces, and intended hurling an irresistable force against us in the spring, and crush Lee's army during the summer. The Northern people were encouraged, the war department took on new life and vigor. President Lincoln promised to furnish everything in the shape of men and means that the Lieutenant-General might ask for.

These gigantic preparations were enough to appal the heart of Gen. Lee, and frighten his half-starved, half-clothed army out of their wits. But nobody seemed to be scared and we pursued the even tenor of our way, preparing to meet the hosts of Grant.

# XXVIII

## The Wilderness and Spotsylvania

The snows are at last gone, and the earth is drying rapidly, and the unmistakable evidences of springtime are beginning to show themselves. The birds are twittering in the pines, the buttercups and daisies are showing their bright faces on every side, and we know that winter is gone.

Soon orders are sent down to us to begin to strip ourselves and have our baggage in condition to be shipped back to our depots in Richmond at a moment's warning. These orders created considerable excitement, and we go to work in earnest, packing our winter goods, and camp conveniences that we cannot carry on the march. The first day of May we shipped our baggage, reserving only such things as we have learned from experience that we must have on the march, to protect ourselves from the changes of the weather, and cook our scant rations. May 3d, three days rations are issued and ordered to be cooked and tents are struck at daylight next morning.

About 8 a.m. we fall into line and bidding adieu to our demolished huts, to our dear old Chapel, where we had heard so many glorious sermons, enjoyed so many precious seasons of prayer and praise, we take the plank road, and start for that strange looking country—The Wilderness, to throw our half-fed soldiers 30,000 or 40,000 strong, against the 140,000 well fed and admirably equipped soldiers of Gen. Grant.[1] What an unequal contest! Yet the veterans of Lee marched cheerfully down the plank road and into that terrible wilderness, where you could not see twenty paces ahead of you, and boldly attacked the foe.

From the evening of the 5th to the 7th the conflict raged all along the lines. In front of Hill's corps, which was formed across the plank road, the Federals seemed to make their chief point of attack. The fighting was done with the musket, no artillery being used on either side, owing to the dense growth of timber and undergrowth. My own regiment lost its Major, Wm. Feeney,[2] who was the last of our field officers who came with the regiment to Virginia in May 1862. He was a brave, kind man, and greatly beloved by his men and subordinate officers. He had been absent for months, recovering from a severe wound received at Gettysburg, and had only recently returned to his regiment. He fell early in the action.

All the evening of the 5th Hill's corps withstood the attack of thousands hurled against them by the Lieutenant-General and advanced his lines several hundred yards, and slept on their arms during the night, in line.

Early on the morning of the 6th I was ordered by the Division Surgeon, Hubbard, to repair to the hospital, eight miles in the rear, on the plank road, and report to Dr. [Hunter C.] McGuire[3] for duty.

When I reached the plank road, I found Longstreet's corps pressing on to the field, to relieve Hill's corps, which had been fighting all the day before. Gens. Lee and Longstreet were riding together and talking earnestly.

It seems that Gen. Lee thought the crisis had arrived, and a desperate effort must be made to drive back the enemy, who was following Hill, who was falling back to give place to Longstreet. Hood's division was rapidly formed, and Gen. Lee proposed to lead it in a charge on the rapidly advancing enemy. The men refused to move. The order was given the second time, and still the men refused to obey. An old soldier stepped out of the lines, and taking Traveler by the bridle, said respectfully:

"Gen. Lee, go to the rear out of danger, and we will drive the enemy back."

A shout of approval went up from the lines, and Gen. Lee, very much moved by this evidence of the devotion of his soldiers, suffered the old Texan to lead Traveler to the rear, then raising the Rebel Yell, Hood's old division charged the advancing foe, drove them back and regained all lost ground.[4]

Bringing his other divisions into action, Longstreet wrestled with the enemy throughout the day, and finally drove them from the field. All morning the roar of musketry gave evidence of the terrible contest going on in the Wilderness, which increased toward noon, and continued throughout the day. In the afternoon the woods caught fire, and another horror was added to the contest, and we were told that many hundreds of the enemy's wounded were burned to death, and probably some of our own. The Federal loss in this battle was 17,666, Lee's less than half that number.[5]

I had a terrible walk back to the division hospital on the plank road, meeting Longstreet's men, Ordnance and Commissary wagons, and several batteries of Artillery. I had to take to the woods more than half the way. Dr. McGuire had everything in readiness, and we went to work with a will, and we had all we could do for thirty hours in operative surgery, amputation and resections, and every variety of gunshot wounds.

About noon of the 7th, Dr. McGuire received orders to join his command, and I was left in charge with orders to finish all operations and ship the wounded on to Richmond as soon as possible, and follow the army, which was on the move, and rejoin my command.

By noon of the 8th I finished my job, and in company with one of our band men, Pierce, started on after the army. We walked down the plank road toward the battlefield, nearly to the point where the first day's fighting occurred, and I suppose we met over one hundred Federal soldiers with their guns, cartridge boxes, and blankets, going to the rear, hunting someone to surrender to. They were in squads of from five to twenty and only three or four of them could make their wants known. They were all foreigners, and a low grade of foreigners at that. Some of them made signs to us, and I don't suppose they had been in America a month. They were perfectly satisfied, and I have no doubt they were grossly deceived, and put into service. Bought, or probably forced into service.

"Pierce," said I, "we are fighting the world. Do you see it? We have met and passed men representing a dozen different nationalities. Not an Englishman, Irishman or Frenchman in the number, and I don't believe there is a German among them. They are the very scum of creation."

When we reached the edge of the battlefield, we found a squadron of Cavalry on the watch, who directed us how to go, and told us Gen. Lee had gained a great victory, and that Grant had moved off the left, and they supposed was making for Spotsylvania Court House, and advised us to turn to the south, which we did, and walked on until sunset. We came to a small farm house, and found a woman milking, which suggested supper, and probably a glass of milk.

"Pierce, let us roost right here tonight. We can't find our regiment in the night, and I am broken down. If you will go down and order supper, I will foot the bill, and I will make a fire while you are gone."

I soon had a fire burning, and Pierce reported that supper would be ready in half an hour. After enjoying a good supper of bread, milk and butter, we returned to our fire in the grove, raked us up a good bed of leaves, and were soon fast asleep. Some time during the night, Pierce waked me, saying:

"Listen, Doctor, the wagons or Artillery have been charging along that road for an hour, and I would like to know what it means."

"Well, we can't find out tonight, Pierce, and we had just as well sleep on till daylight."

But it was impossible to go to sleep. We had become uneasy, so we got up and kindled our fire, ate the last of our rations as we had nothing else to do, and talked on, it seemed to us, for ages. At last I saw a light in the farm house, so I knew the widow was up, so I went down to see if I could learn anything. I found the wagons were on the Orange and Spotsylvania road, and going toward Spotsylvania. This was all right. The good woman told me she would give us breakfast at daylight, so I went back and relieved Pierce, and turned in for another nap. At daylight we ate a hearty breakfast, and started toward Spotsylvania, and about 10 o'clock we stumbled upon our brigade headquarters, and found our regiment falling in line to go out in quest of the enemy.

Before we had gone very far we flushed the enemy and had a running fight for three or four miles. The fighting was all done by the sharpshooters, the brigade following at a safe distance. We had none killed or wounded, but the sharpshooters killed several, among them an officer, in whose pocket was found a well written diary, which the soldiers gave me that night.

This diary I kept during the war and in June '65 mailed it to the officer's wife in Seneca, N. Y., and in time received a nicely written letter, thanking me for the diary, and the information I gave in regard to her husband's death. The fighting so far amounted only to skirmishing, as each side selected its lines and began entrenching for the great contest. The Confederates were poorly supplied with tools, in fact they had none, except such imperfect implements as their native ingenuity devised. Consequently their entrenchments and breastworks were very inferior as compared to the Federals, who had a splendid Pioneer corps, and were supplied with an abundance of the best entrenching tools.

Gen. Grant assaulted our lines at different places for five days without making any impression, or gaining any advantage.

On the morning of the fifth day Gen. Hancock's corps made a desperate assault and carried a salient in their front and captured Gen. Edward Johnson and 3,000 or 4,000 prisoners with a battery of artillery.[6]

This was a terrible disaster and our army seemed to be in imminent danger of being cut in two, but our men rallied, fresh troops were hurried to the center and the blue wave of invaders were driven back into the bloody angle where the conflict raged until darkness put an end to the contest. A new and stronger line was formed and the Federals only had a small portion of the angle captured in the morning.

Thus ended the terrible battle of Spotsylvania. No material advantage had been gained. Three thousand prisoners and twenty pieces of artillery had been captured but at the terrible sacrifice of over 20,000 Federal soldiers. The Lieutenant-General had been in command of the Army of the Potomac about three weeks, and had lost in that short space of time about 40,000 men. And still the Army of North Virginia is intact. Morale good and nobody frightened. Men never fought better, or more stubbornly than Lee's soldiers in these battles, Wilderness and Spotsylvania.[7]

Each man was a hero, and acquitted himself as such. But there was one act of gallantry performed by one scarcely more than a boy that deserves to be placed on record and I have never seen it in print. Such an act of gallantry in the days of chivalry would have won knighthood.

App Hancock, a Mississippi boy, a member of Co. J, 19th Mississippi regiment, was acting as courier for Gen. Nat Harris, whose brigade was in that terrible bloody angle. The General wished to send an order to his brigade to come out, and instructions how to come out.

He called for young Hancock.

"I wish this order to be taken to my brigade, if they get it they can save themselves, if they do not get it they will certainly be captured. I will not order you to take it to them, it would be ordering you to death."

App Hancock took the order, and looking for a moment to decide the safest course to reach the brigade, sprang upon the breastworks and ran upon the top of the parapet the whole distance and, springing into the ditch among the men, delivered the order and saved the brigade. He never received a scratch although a thousand bullets were fired at him at close range. A marvelous escape. A most gallant act of devotion to duty.[8]

The dispatches of the Lieutenant-General to his government about the time sounded rather ridiculous to an old Confederate in the ditches, and caused a grim smile to light up his countenance. They were something like this:

"Father Abraham:—

I have lost about 40,000 of your brave men in the last three weeks, and have not accomplished much, but I intend to fight it out on this line if it takes me all summer. So send on the men."

Unwilling to risk another assault upon the Confederate lines around Spotsylvania, the Lieutenant-General turned to the left and made for Hanover Junction, where he again found Lee's ragged rebels across his pathway. At this place there was some fighting or skirmishing but nothing like a battle until Gen. Grant attacked our army, occupying McClellan's old entrenchments at Cold Harbor.

Will he rout Gen. Lee, as Jackson did McClellan in 1862?

We will see.

# XXIX

## Cold Harbor, Petersburg, and Appomattox

———————◆▶▶———————

There was considerable preliminary fighting all along the Cold Harbor lines June 2d, but on the 3d, Gen. Grant having received heavy reinforcements, made a determined assault on the Confederate position, receiving one of the bloodiest repulses of the war.

Swinton, the Northern historian of the Army of the Potomac, says of this battle, that it was decided in an incredibly short space of time, and the Federals lost over 13,000 men, and that when another charge was ordered, "no man stirred, and the immobile lines pronounced a verdict, silent yet emphatic, against further slaughter."[1]

My own recollections of this battle do not accord with Prof. Swinton. There was heavy fighting all along the lines, and many determined assaults at different points. In front of Gen. Breckinridge's division the Federals gained some slight advantage, capturing a salient and one or two hundred prisoners of Finegan's Florida brigade, and wounded Gen. Breckinridge. This was a mile or more south, or to the right of Gen. Lee's center, where I suppose the slaughter spoken of by Swinton occurred, which was in front of Hill's corps, who always held the center, and whose lines were never broken.

Our loss was trifling, considerably less than a thousand, in killed and wounded. In fact so few wounded had been brought in by dark, that the regimental surgeons

176

were ordered to visit their commands in person, and see that the wounded had all been brought off.

In company with my little corps, I reached our intrenchments about 10 o'clock, and walked through the ditches, the entire length of the brigade, congratulating the friends I found awake. It was the first time I had ever been on the lines in the night, and it was a strange and novel scene. About two-thirds of the men were asleep. Fast asleep! Lying in every conceivable position, propped up or leaning against the breastworks, or lying in the ditch, with a cartridge box or blanket for a pillow. The others were watching closely the enemy's breastworks, and firing on anything that looked like a soldier above the breastworks, and every man, asleep or awake, clasping his Enfield rifle. Glorious fellows! Well may your country be proud of you!

The Federal breastworks seemed to be about 200 yards away, and although there was no moonlight, could be discerned as well as the level space between, which seemed to be pretty thickly strewn with dead and wounded men, many of whom were calling piteously for water and help. The sharpshooting was going on, though not an active fire. At last I reached the 42d Miss. and found the boys all right, no killed or wounded. I had not seen them for several days, and it required some time to go through, shake hands and ask after each one. I finally reached Capt. A. M. Nelson,[2] who was in command of the regiment. After shaking hands and congratulating him on being alive, he said to me:

"I am very thankful we have all escaped, but when the blue wave swept over those breastworks, yonder, and started across that space, I thought our chances were very

177

slim, but we succeeded in driving them back, and the ground out there is nearly covered with their dead and wounded, and it is really distressing to hear those poor fellows out there crying for water and help."

While we were talking, three men came up in haste, and excitedly asked us to go with them down the lines a short distance. We followed the men in silence, wondering what they wanted. After going about 100 yards, they stopped, and said:

"Keep still now and listen."

Presently a wail came up from that battlefield that chilled our blood, and caused our hearts to stand still. Words none of us ever heard outside of a lodge of Master Masons.

"Did you hear that Captain? Give us permission to go and get that man."

"I can't do that boys. I would be court-martialed if I did. You know your duty."

"Well, Captain, you and the Doctor go up and down the lines, and tell the men not to shoot us."

"All right."

And as these three brave men crawled over the breastworks, we started in different directions, warning the men, and returned to the spot and anxiously awaited the return of the soldiers. Soon we heard them coming, and with very pleasant feelings we helped the men lift the wounded Federal over the breastworks. He was severely wounded, and was famishing for water. He was very grateful, and said we had saved his life. After supplying his wants, I had him carried out to the hospital, dressed his wounds, and next morning sent him in to Richmond, to the city hospital.

On the 4th or 5th, Gen. Grant asked permission to bury his dead, and Gen. Lee granted a truce of two hours for that purpose.[3] I went out to the lines to witness this strange scene, for a strange scene it certainly was. At 2 p.m. a cannon fired on the right, and was immediately followed by one on the left. Then white flags were run up on our breastworks, and then the strange proceedings commenced.

Over the breastworks went Rebel and Yank, and met between the lines, and commenced laughing and talking, and you would have thought that old friends had met after a long separation. Some were talking earnestly together, some swapping coffee for tobacco, some were wrestling, some boxing, others trading knives. The Pioneer corps were burying the dead, and hustling them into the ground as rapidly as possible. The dead were terribly swollen, and as black as an Ethiopian and it was really a horrible scene.

In a short time the boom of a cannon on the right, followed by one on the left, announced the truce at an end.

"Good-by, Reb!"

"Good-by, Yank!"

And the men scampered to their places inside the breastworks, the white flags disappeared, and the sharp-shooting commenced.

The Federal soldiers seemed to care very little for their dead comrades, in fact they paid no attention to the burying going on that day. This was the first time that Gen. Grant had asked permission to bury his dead, and I think he had paid very little attention to this respectable portion of his vast army.

For two or three days longer the armies confronted

each other. Gen. Grant seemed to be perfectly satisfied and no more assaults were made upon the Cold Harbor lines, and he commenced moving by his favorite left flank.

The next blow was struck at Petersburg, 22 miles south of Richmond. When his advanced guard reached that place they were met by Gen. Beauregard in command of the old men and boys of that city, and were repulsed and driven back.[4]

Before a sufficient force arrived to capture the city, Lee's veterans had entered the breastworks and were ready to receive them.

And now comes the siege of Petersburg.[5] I suppose it was the latter part of June before any considerable portion of Grant's army was transferred to the south of the James river. One or two considerable efforts were made to break the lines in front of the city of Petersburg, which signally failed, and then the Lieutenant-General went to mining to try and blow up the works he couldn't carry by assault. He had failed to run over Lee's army above ground, and he would now try to crawl under. Gen. Lee, of course, commenced counter-mining; and also constructed an inner line of works to be used in case the enemy succeeded in blowing us up.

Hill's corps was still north of the James and we could hear a great deal about this mining effort and it kept us continually uneasy because it was something new. A new departure in military tactics as far as this army was concerned. I suppose every soldier in our army expected something new when the "Hero from the West" was placed in command of the Army of the Potomac, but so far it was the same old thing, hammer and rapier, fight and kill. With this significant difference, Gen. Grant always had more than one live man to put in the place of the dead one. 70,000 had been placed hors de combat since he crossed the Rappahanock in May with 150,000, now he has 200,000 investing Petersburg. But Lee's veterans had been fighting odds so long, numbers had no significance to them. They had implicit confidence in their Generals, their Generals had implicit confidence in their men. Glorious leaders! Glorious soldiers! Xenophones' celebrated 10,000 cannot be compared to them in loyalty, endurance and valor.

About July 29th our brigade, which had been gradually moving to the right from the Cold Harbor lines, or battlefield, and was now in the neighborhood of Deep Bottom, north of the James river, was suddenly ordered to Petersburg.

We were hurried across the country to a point on the Richmond and Petersburg R. R. where a train of box cars awaited us. The day was fearfully hot, and the rapid marching produced many cases of prostration. The first cases we had had during the campaign. Fortunately none proved fatal.

We reached Petersburg about 5 p.m. and found Gen. Heth's aide-de-camp waiting at the depot for us. Instead of leading us out to the lines he put us in camp very near the depot with orders for every man to be kept in camp ready to fall into line at a moment's notice.

It had been rumored that the mine was ready and might be fired at any moment, and there was no telling at what point on the lines an assault might be made, so we were held as a reserve to be used as circumstances demanded.

About sunrise the next morning, July 30th, the shock

181

came. It was not a loud report, as we expected, but a low rumbling report with a slight quivering of the earth, like a faint earthquake. Instantly the brigade was called into line and ready to march.

An aide-de-camp galloped up and hurriedly marched us across the city and into the breastworks, a mile or more south, or to the right of the blow-up. As soon as the mine was sprung, or fired, the Federals forced a corps of negro soldiers across the space between the lines, which was not more than one hundred yards wide, into the Confederate lines.

A battery of four or six pieces, and probably sixty or eighty yards of our breastworks had been blown up, leaving an immense crater or excavation in the earth. Into this crater and the deserted breastworks the negro troops crowded, trying to protect themselves from the bullets of the Confederates. The white troops of Gen. Grant failed to put in an appearance, the Artillery on either side of the blow up was turned diagonally across that field between the lines, and nothing living could pass or repass. A brigade of Virginians was sent in to recapture the lines, and either killed or captured all those negroes. The dead were thrown into the crater, and the negro prisoners required to fill it up, and the works were rebuilt by these prisoners and ready to be occupied before night. Our loss was reported to be 275 killed, wounded and missing. The Federal loss was reported to be about 5,000. The new departure did not pan out.[6]

Mining did not pay.

Nothing is said of this mining experiment of Gen. Grant in [James] Redpath's History,[7] nor is it mentioned in a condensed school history I have kept by me to refer to as to dates and names, and I have written it from memory, just as I have everything else. Neither do I find mention made of the shelling of Petersburg, which occurred shortly after.

Why Gen. Grant should turn his batteries loose on a city during the hours of night, without giving warning to the authorities, or time to remove the women and children, I have never seen explained. It was a strange act for an American General. He must have been terribly mortified at the result of his mining effort and the loss of his negro troops. Over one thousand shells were dropped into this city by the mortar batteries and other guns, and strange to tell, little or no damage was done to the city, and not one white person killed or injured, but four old and three young negroes were killed in the eastern part of the city.

Gen. Grant continued to move to the left, or rather extended his lines to the left, and many brilliant sorties were made upon them by our men, but there was no important engagement until the 20th of August, when Gen. Hill gained a handsome victory over Hancock's corps, near Reams' Station, on the Weldon railroad, capturing over 3,000 prisoners.[8]

When the prisoners were marched through Petersburg they made quite a show and considerable excitement and rejoicing among our people. I suppose it was the first time the people of Petersburg had ever seen any Federal prisoners, and they were out on the sidewalks to witness the show.

My regiment, the 42d Miss., had nineteen wounded in this engagement. None killed.[9]

Two of our wounded died from their wounds. One case was so remarkable I will give a short history of it for the benefit of any surgeon or doctor who may read this.

John Davis, ball passed through the abdomen mid-way between the navel and pubis striking the spine, causing complete paralysis of the lower limbs. I saw and examined him about 9 p.m. I found him suffering intensely although I had sent him two large doses of morphine. Urine bloody and constant desire to pass it, surface cold and clammy. I decided it was a mortal wound and the man would die before morning, and to relieve his intense suffering I gave him 10 grains of morphine in whisky, and returned to my work. It was 12 m. before we got through with the wounded, many of whom were brought in after dark. After getting through with the Federal wounded that had been sent me as my share, I went round to see how my boys were doing, I found John Davis fast asleep and, I supposed taking his last nap.

Next morning I found him alive, perfectly comfortable and wanting his breakfast.

We sent the wounded to the city hospital and I was so much interested in John Davis that I went with him, and talked his case over with the surgeon in charge, and visited him regularly. He lived twenty-nine days. The tissues about the sacrum and buttocks all sloughed off before death, the result of extravasation of urine.

How did this man escape peritonitis?

Why did not the morphine kill him?

The first question I cannot answer. I know the minnie ball passed directly through the abdomen from front to rear.

Second question—the man was suffering such intense agony that it required just 12 grains of morphine to relieve the pain.

How do you like my answer, Doctor?

Gen. Grant again extended his line, and we had quite an engagement at Hatcher's Run.[10] My own brigade was not in this fight, and I can only say that the enemy was driven back with considerable loss. There was one very sad event connected with it which cast a gloom over a large portion of the army. Brig. Gen. Ingraham, a remarkably fine looking and gallant officer, from Baltimore, who had been married but a few hours to Miss Cary, of Richmond, was killed. His body was borne to the P. & R. depot by a squad of soldiers and many friends, where it was met by his young wife of a day, and friends from Richmond, and I witnessed a scene of sorrow, such as only "horrid war" can produce.

About October 1st, Gen. Wade Hampton, in command of Gen. Stuart's cavalry, made a raid in the rear of Grant's army, and drove back 2,500 fine fat northern beeves, which caused a smile to pass over the stomachs of Lee's hungry veterans. It was certainly the prettiest sight I ever saw. Beef went down.

Nothing of interest or importance occurred on the lines for some time, and we began to prepare for winter quarters. Our hospital department was moved from the place we had occupied south of the city, in the suburbs, some distance across the Appomattox river, in a westerly course from the city, for the benefit of water, fuel, and material to build our winter huts. Here we soon made ourselves very comfortable. Everything was different from what it was a year ago. Our men are more than three miles away from us; then we had them with us, all around us, in camp.

I soon found we were going to have a lonesome time.

I had been given an assistant surgeon, whose duties kept him with the men on the lines. It was the best for me, but I had much rather have been with my men. John Powell was at home, recovering from a wound, which would probably cripple him for life.[11] Chaplain Witherspoon, also, who had been my messmate after John Powell was wounded, changed his quarters to the lines, and I was deprived of his valued company and companionship, and we only had a small community of surgeons.

For mutual improvement and pleasure we formed a medical society, and passed many pleasant hours, discussing medical and surgical subjects. We had a regular dissecting hut out in the pine thicket, built and fitted up by Dr. Holt, surgeon of the 2d Miss. regiment. We could easily procure subjects from "beyond the lines," and we thought it legitimate to use them for scientific and educational purposes.

In this way we improved ourselves, and passed the time away. Christmas came and passed, and we hardly knew it. It was very different from the jolly good time we had a year ago. We missed the minstrels and their fine music. We made it a rule, or the Brigade Surgeon ordered, that one of the surgeons should visit the lines every day, which we did through the winter, and it was quite a pleasure, unless the weather was very bitter. We attended services on the lines, and occasionally visited the churches.

Thus the winter passed slowly away. Rations were getting scarcer and privations increasing day by day. Strange to tell, I hear no grumbling, I see no wavering, I witness no despondency among officers or men. The same old unconquerable spirit pervades the rank and file. They have been and are making the great struggle for constitutional freedom, and the spirit of 1776 lives again in the sons of the sires, and they cry:

"Give me liberty or give me death!"

When Col. L. J. C. Lawson, returning from Fortress Monroe, where the Peace Commission had gone to confer with Mr. Lincoln and Mr. Seward on the subject, and learn their terms; called us around him he told us we had no friends, we had nothing to hope for. The only terms offered through Mr. Seward were:

"Lay down your arms, and we will then offer terms."

That was enough to appal the hearts of Lee's ragged soldiers, but what do I hear, a shout goes up:

"That's enough, Colonel, that is enough, we'll fight them till h——l freezes over and then meet them on the ice!"

But the end must come, the enemy begin to move, the lines of the veterans begin to stretch out and continue to stretch until they break, and the lines held for ten long months must be evacuated.

And now the lines have been so stretched, the field has become so large, that a Confederate surgeon can't take in the situation, and you must allow me to quote from our beloved Chaplain General's admirable School History of the United States:[12]

"An immense line was held all day against repeated efforts to break it, but Lee saw that evacuation was now necessary, and that morning sent the famous telegram to Mr. Davis, which was delivered while he was quietly worshipping in St. Paul's church, Richmond, of which he was a member, and was received, and treated with the calm dignity and indomitable courage which so characterized the Confederate President. Preparations were made for

187

evacuating the whole line that night. The President and his officials took a train of cars for Danville, bearing themselves as proudly in defeat as they had done in victory, and that night the silent columns of gray moved out on roads leading to Danville."

Only two incidents connected with the fall of Richmond and Petersburg will be given here:[13]

Lieut.-Gen. A. P. Hill, one of the most gallant and skillful soldiers of the army with which he had been identified from the beginning, on hearing that his lines had been broken, was attempting to reach the part of the corps that had been cut off, was shot and instantly killed by a vidette of the enemy whom he attempted to capture. Able, accomplished, brave and patriotic, he had been one of the most conspicuous figures in the Army of Northern Virginia and had rendered the Confederacy most devoted and valuable service.

In the campaign of 1864 his corps had killed, wounded and captured double as many men as it numbered, and had taken in battle a number of guns, flags, etc., without ever having his line broken, or losing a gun or flag. And now its superb leader fell in the hour of disaster, when his lines for the first time had been broken, the grand old army he had contributed so much to make, about to go to pieces, and the cause he loved so well, about to fail.

The other incident is the heroic defense of Ft. Gregg, an enclosed work on the right of Lee's lines, into which detachments of the 12th and 16th Miss. regiments of Harris' brigade, some Artillerymen of Hill's corps, and a few others of different commands, had retreated, and which they defended with an obstinate courage and self-sacrificing devotion, worthy to be written alongside the most heroic achievements of history, forming a fitting close to the grand defense of Petersburg.

Gen. Lee's plan now was to concentrate his army at Amelia Court House, where he had ordered rations to be collected, and then using the Richmond & Danville railroad to transfer his army to the south to unite with Johnston and strike Sherman.

But when he reached Amelia Court House he found that his orders had not been carried out, and no rations had been collected. The day's delay, trying to collect rations from the surrounding country, proved fatal, as it enabled Grant to cut the railroad south of him, and then began that running fight between overwhelming odds of the enemy and Lee's ragged, weary, starving remnant of his glorious old army, which fight terminated at Appomattox.

On the 7th of April Gen. Grant wrote Lee, suggesting his surrender, and the famous correspondence between them ensued, and on the same date his corps commanders suggested to Lee that the time for negotiations had come. Longstreet and Gordon commanded the Infantry; Fitz Lee was chief of Cavalry and Pendleton the chief of Artillery.

On the night of the 8th it was agreed that early the next morning Gordon and Fitz Lee should advance toward Appomattox station, and cut their way through if nothing but cavalry barred the road, and that Longstreet should follow, but, if Gen. Grant's infantry was up in full force, they should call a halt and notify Gen. Lee, who would raise a flag of truce and seek Gen. Grant, with a view to surrender.

Accordingly the next morning Gordon and Fitz Lee advanced, drove Sheridan handsomely, captured two pieces of Artillery and a number of prisoners. But their victorious advance was finally checked by Gen. Ord and two corps of Federal infantry, numbering 40,000 men.

In a word, Gen. Lee, with a force that had dwindled down to barely 7,800 men with arms in their hands, was surrounded by about 80,000 Federals, and surrender was inevitable. When the message of the chivalric Gordon came—

"Tell Gen. Lee I have fought my old corps to a frazzle and can do nothing more, unless heavily supported by Longstreet,"

General Lee said:

"Then there is nothing left me but to go to Gen. Grant and I had rather die a thousand deaths than to do it."[14]

But Gen. Grant's terms were generous, and his whole bearing on the occasion, chivalric. The two chiefs met at Appomattox Court House, in the parlor of Mr. [Major Wilmer] McLean, whose house on Bull Run Beauregard had for his headquarters during the fight of the 18th of July, 1861, and the occasion was marked by calm dignity and manly bearing on both sides.

When Gen. Lee returned to his headquarters from his meeting with Gen. Grant, officers and men crowded around him to take his hand, and bronzed veterans of an hundred glorious victories wept like children, that the Cause they loved, and for which they would gladly have laid down their lives, had failed. Gen. Lee issued to his army the following farewell:

190

HEADQUARTERS ARMY OF NORTHERN VIRGINIA,
April 10th, 1865.

After four years of arduous service, marked by unsur-
passed courage and fortitude, the Army of Northern
Virginia has been compelled to yield to overwhelming
numbers and resources. I need not tell the [brave] survivors of so many hard fought battles, who have remained
steadfast to the last, that I have consented to this result
from no distrust in them; but feeling that valor and devotion could accomplish nothing that could compensate for
the loss that would have attended the continuation [con-
tinuence] of the contest, I have determined to avoid the
useless sacrifice of those whose past services have
endeared them to their countrymen. By the terms of the
agreement, officers and men can return to their homes and
remain there until exchanged. You will take with you the
satisfaction that proceeds from the consciousness of duty
faithfully performed; and I earnestly pray that a Merciful
God will extend to you His blessing and protection. With
an inceasing admiration of your constancy and devotion
to your Country, and a grateful remembrance of your kind
and generous consideration for myself, I bid you an
affectionate farewell.

R. E. LEE, Genl.[15]

There was, of course, general rejoicing among the
victors, but there was no firing of salutes, no cheering, no

manifestations that could wound the feelings of the conquered. To the credit of "the men blue," be it said that they respected the men with whom they had fought so long, and treated them with the highest consideration.

And thus the Army of the Potomac and the Army of Northern Virginia marched into history.

# Notes

## CHAPTER I

1. Wilson's company, The Alcorn Rifles, was Company F of the First Regiment, Mississippi Volunteers, Army of Tennessee. It was mustered into Confederate service at Iuka on August 28, 1861. The men enlisted for twelve months at Hopkinsville, Kentucky, on September 19, 1861. Of the 74 men enrolled, eleven were killed in battle and eleven died from other causes. The officers were: Captain J. J. Milam, 1st Lt. L. J. Wilson, 2nd Lt. William D. Howze, 3rd Lt. M. L. Mobley.

2. A thriving community six miles northwest of Chulahoma, 16 miles west of Holly Springs. A military "affair" was reported to have taken place at Wall Hill on February 12, 1864. In the 1870's the town contained a school, Masonic lodge, stores, and many houses. At that time two merchants each purchased annually more than a thousand bales of cotton which were hauled the sixty miles to Memphis in ox wagons. People moved away during the drouth years of the early 1880's, and today Wall Hill is only a name on the map.

3. James Wilson, fourth son of Robert and Clara Wilson, was born April 6, 1791 in Dinwiddie County, Virginia, and died November 6, 1871, near Tyro, Mississippi. He is buried in the family cemetery near Wall Hill, Mississippi. Dr. Wilson's mother died May 1, 1861. In the family Bible are written these words: "Elizabeth Joseph Wilson departed this life . . . after a life of persevering industry and economy, in full reliance of the Christian hope." They had been married 47 years.

4. Elizabeth Carey Skipwith Wilson. According to Dr. Wilson, "These were dark days of trial, and I could see that my young wife was suffering intensely. One day I told her I was ashamed to stay at home any longer. She said with firm but trembling voice, 'Husband, if you think it is your duty to go into the army *now*, go. You must discharge your duty.' "

5. Frank Small Wilson died in 1876 at the age of fifteen.

6. Thou turnest man to destruction,
And sayest, Return, ye children of men.
For a thousand years in thy sight
Are but as yesterday when it is past,
And as a watch in the night.
Thou carriest them away as with a flood; they are as a sleep:
In the morning they are like grass which groweth up.
In the morning it flourisheth, and groweth up;
In the evening it is cut down, and withereth.

. . . . . . . . . . . . . .

And let the favor of the Lord our God be upon us. , , ,
7. Captain Jackson J. Milam, from Wall Hill, was commissioned on July 29, 1861. He was 40 years old. After the surrender of Port Hudson he was imprisoned at Johnson Island.


## CHAPTER II

1. In the 1st Mississippi Regiment were ten companies and 682 men. Field officers were Colonel John M. Simonton, Lieutenant Colonel A. S. Hamilton, and Major Thomas H. Johnston. Its camp of instruction was set up at Iuka in August, 1861. It was one of four regiments sent to General Albert Sidney Johnston by Governor John J. Pettus. In Kentucky it was brigaded with the 8th Kentucky, the 3rd Mississippi, and the 7th Texas. At Fort Donelson there were 331 present, 16 of whom were killed and 61 wounded. Most, of course, surrendered. After the exchange the 1st Mississippi reported to Meridian on October 26, 1862, and was sent in January, 1863 to Port Hudson, Louisiana, where it surrendered on July 9, 1863.

The initial organization of the First Mississippi was:

| Company | Name | Mustered in |
|---------|------|-------------|
| A | Walker Reserves | May 7 |
| B | Mooresville Darts | August 28 |
| C | Reube Davis Rifles | August 2 |
| D | DeSoto Grays | August 27 |
| E | Pleasant Mount Rifles | July 25 |
| F | Alcorn Rifles | August 28 |
| G | Dave Rogers Rifles | September 9 |
| H | James Creek Volunteers | September 3 |
| I | Rifle Scouts | July 8 |
| K | Mississippi Yankee Hunters | August 28 |

| Captain | County |
|---------|--------|
| George M. Moseley | Marshall |
| Merriman Pounds | Itawamba |
| William Young | Pontotoc |
| W. J. Boone | DeSoto |
| M. W. Wilborn | Panola |
| J. J. Milam | Marshall |
| L. M. Laushe | LaFayette |
| J. Furgerson | Itawamba |
| J. M. Simonton | Itawamba |
| A. S. Hamilton | Itawamba |

194

2. United States prison camp four miles south of Columbus, Ohio.

3. United States prison camp in Sandusky Bay, Ohio.

4. Field officers were elected September 10, 1861, with John M. Simonton as colonel. Born in Lawrence County, Tennessee, June 17, 1830, Simonton engaged in the mercantile business in Carmengo, Mississippi, after 1850. He was in the Mississippi Senate from 1859 to 1861, and again in 1864-1868, after his resignation from the army in October, 1863. He attended the 1890 Mississippi Constitutional Convention, was made state land commissioner in 1895, and died three years later.

5. Elected captain on August 2, 1861, Hamilton was 38 years old. He died at Johnson's Island November 2, 1863.

6. Thomas H. Johnston (Dr. Wilson always seemed to leave out the "t" from the name Johnston) was later promoted to lieutenant colonel and commanded the regiment at Port Hudson.

7. The DeSoto Grays.

8. Probably Captain Boone of Company D.

9. Later (1869-71) governor of Mississippi, Alcorn had been appointed in January, 1861, one of the four brigadier generals in the Army of Mississippi. At this time he was organizing troops for service in Kentucky.

10. William Joseph Hardee's *Rifle and Light Infantry Tactics*, published in 1856, the basic infantry manual for both Union and Confederate armies.

## CHAPTER III

1. This was probably Brooks (Presbyterian) Chapel at Chulahoma.

2. Hopkinsville is 64 miles west of Bowling Green. But if Wilson traveled by way of Russelville (29 miles) and Clarksville, Tennessee, this roundabout journey took him about ninety miles. Hopkinsville is 27 miles directly north of Clarksville.

3. Alcorn's Brigade was composed of the 1st and 3rd Mississippi, the 9th Texas, and the 4th Kentucky regiments.

## CHAPTER IV

1. The 1st Mississippi officially reported at Hopkinsville on October 10, 1861. General Alcorn commanded about 1700 infantry, armed with shotguns. The men were destined for little fighting in 1861 but suffered intensely from measles and pneumonia. Alcorn's regiments were disbanded at the expiration of the sixty-day term of enlistments, but most of the men re-enlisted.

2. George M. Moseley, captain of Company A, the Walker Reserves, was severely wounded at Gettysburg. See Chapter XV, footnote 2 and Chapter XXI, footnote 15.

3. Eleven men of the 1st Regiment were buried in Hopkinsville.

## CHAPTER V

1. Rufus K. Byrd, 4th sergeant, Company F, was 37 years old when he died in Hopkinsville in November, 1861.

2. Lieutenant William Duke Howze, 23 years old, was a younger brother of George Adrian Howze (see Chapter XXI, footnote 3). He enlisted with his uncle, Dr. Wilson, in the 1st Mississippi Regiment and commanded the Alcorn Rifles at Donelson. He was taken prisoner and exchanged in 1862. There were two other Howze brothers in the Confederate service. James Wilson Howze enlisted at the age of 16 in the 19th Mississippi Regiment and was mortally wounded in the Chickahominy Swamp. The youngest brother, Henry LeGrande Howze, joined the 1st Mississippi Regiment when it was exchanged in 1863. He was in the defense of Port Hudson where he was captured. Paroled and sent home, Henry was taken by a Federal raiding party from Memphis, despite his plea that he was only hunting squirrels. He was imprisoned and then sent to Camp Chase for the rest of the war.

3. Surgeon G. H. Hall, 1st Lieutenant, Company 4, 1st Mississippi Regiment.

4. Dr. J. L. Raiford, 1st Lieutenant, Pleasant Mount Rifles, resigned October 17, 1861.

5. Sergeant Archibald S. Yarbrough was later promoted to assistant surgeon.

6. Charles Clark, veteran of the Mexican War, was one of Mississippi's four brigadiers, appointed in January, 1861. Later wounded at Shiloh and Baton Rouge, Clark became Mississippi's governor in the fall of 1863.

## CHAPTER VI

1. From the pen of Major General Lew Wallace:

"The village of Dover was—and for that matter yet is—what our English cousins would call the "shiretown" of the county of Stewart, Tennessee. In 1860 it was a village unknown to fame, meager in population, architecturally poor. There was a court-house in the place, and a tavern, remembered now as double-storied, unpainted, and with windows of eight-by-ten glass, which, if the panes may be likened to eyes, were both squint and cataractous. Looking through them gave the street outside the appearance of a sedgy slough of yellow backwater. The enter-

196

tainment furnished man and beast was good of the kind; though at the time mentioned a sleepy traveler, especially if he were of the North, might have been somewhat vexed by the explosions which spiced the good things of a debating society that nightly took possession of the barroom, to discuss the relative fighting qualities of the opposing sections.

"If there was a little of the romantic in Dover itself, there was still less of poetic quality in the country round about it. The only beautiful feature was the Cumberland River, which, in placid current from the south, poured its waters, ordinarily white and pure as those of the springs that fed it, past the village on the east. Northward there was a hill, then a small stream, then a bolder hill round the foot of which the river swept to the west, as if courteously bent on helping Hickman's Creek out of its boggy bottom and cheerless ravine. North of the creek all was woods. Taking in the ravine of the creek, a system of hollows, almost wide and deep enough to be called valleys, inclosed the town and two hills, their bluffest ascents being on the townward side. Westward of the hollows there were woods apparently interminable. From Fort Henry, twelve miles northwest, a road entered the village, stopping first to unite itself with another wagon-way, now famous as the Wynn's Ferry road, coming more directly from the west. Still another road, leading off to Charlotte and Nashville, had been cut across the low ground near the river on the south. These three highways were the chief reliance of the people of Dover for communication with the country, and as they were more than supplemented by the river and its boatage, the three were left the year round to the guardianship of the winds and rains."

2. The Federal gunboats opened on Fort Henry February 5, 1862. The fort was surrendered the next day. General Gideon J. Pillow assigned the 1st Mississippi Regiment to a brigade under Colonel T. J. Davidson, with Lyon's Kentucky and Gregg's Texas regiments.

3. The Federal fleet arrived on February 12, 1862. The 1st Mississippi was in the trenches under Lt. Col. Hamilton. General Grant attacked on February 13. The sally from the works was attempted at midnight, February 14-15, under the command of Colonel Simonton. The 1st Mississippi was marched out at dawn and, seriously engaging General McClernand's Division, fought and won a hill after an hour's fight. It accomplished a second successful charge, advanced over a mile and a half, and was then ordered back to the rifle pits. Of the 331 men in battle, sixteen were killed, 61 wounded, and the rest, except for a few escapees, surrendered. Davidson's brigade lost 68 killed, 218 wounded.

4. Well might Dr. Wilson have been confused by the events of February 15th! The day before the Confederate position had been completely invested; but a Federal assault on the outworks was thrown back and the Union gunboats repulsed. Communication by river was open to

Nashville. By 11 A.M. on February 15 the Confederates had smashed through the Federal lines and opened the road to Nashville. Then southern mismanagement plus gallant Union action reinstated the siege. That night the Confederate surrender was agreed upon.

5. Then a lieutenant-colonel, Forrest attended the midnight conference where it was decided to surrender Donelson. He told General Buckner: "I did not come here for the purpose of surrendering my command." At dawn he led his command up the river road and "out of the trap."

## CHAPTER VIII

1. From five to twelve thousand Confederates surrendered with Fort Donelson. No one knows how many escaped on the Sunday (February 16) of the surrender. According to Stanley Horn, "Some simply walked through the lines and made off," with discipline in both armies at the vanishing point.

2. Dr. William M. Compton, under whom Wilson had "read" medicine for two years after graduating from Union Academy. From Talloola, Compton had organized Company A, the Walker Reserves.

## CHAPTER IX

1. The Federal army reached Nashville on Sunday, February 23, and the city was surrendered the next day.

## CHAPTER X

1. Probably one of the Mississippi treasury notes, issued to the amount of five million dollars, and advanced to the holders of cotton at five cents a pound.

2. On February 16th the Federal gunboats steamed up to Dover. The *Carondelet* immediately returned to Cairo, but Dr. Wilson may have seen the ironclads *Pittsburgh, St. Louis,* and *Louisville,* as well as the wooden gun-boats *Tyler* and *Conestoga.*

3. Famous British steamship, 1859-1887. For many years the largest vessel afloat.

4. Clarksville is about thirty miles east of Dover.

## CHAPTER XI

1. Dover is about twenty miles south of the Kentucky border.

2. If Dr. White's home was in Kentucky, Wilson must have traveled almost due north.

3. Probably Captain Gannaway, Company F, 1st Mississippi Regiment.

4. By his own figures, Dr. Wilson had by this time traveled, probably in a wide semi-circle to the north and east, some fifty miles since leaving Dover.

## CHAPTER XII

1. Clarksville is about fifty miles down the Cumberland River from Nashville.

2. Ashland is about twenty miles northwest and down the Cumberland from Nashville, which Dr. Wilson avoided. The trip as described is perfectly logical, as it is 34 miles from Clarksville to Springfield. By turning south before reaching Springfield, Wilson evaded the Union forces.

3. John H. Morgan was a captain until after Shiloh.

## CHAPTER XIII

1. Franklin is about twenty miles south of Nashville, a little less than half the distance from Nashville to Columbia. The way Dr. Wilson traveled, it was probably about thirty miles from Ashland to Franklin.

2. General Johnston had begun his move south from Murfreesboro on February 28, 1862. By March 18 the head of his column had reached Corinth, Mississippi.

3. Columbia is 24 miles south of Franklin.

4. At Decatur the Tennessee and Alabama Railroad connected with the Memphis and Charleston.

5. Allen Stokes was a captain in the 9th Mississippi Regiment.

6. The 1860 Memphis city directory lists Simpson, Hayes and Company (William S. Simpson, William D. Hayes, and Francis Sanders) as cotton factors and commission merchants at 40 Front Row. George A. Howze was listed as a cotton clerk.

7. See Chapter XXI, footnote 3.

8. Peyton Skipwith was the father of Mrs. Wilson. The *Commercial Appeal* of June 29, 1959, carried an item about the death of Mrs. Annie Skipwith, "widow of the late Peyton Skipwith, Sr., cotton dealer."

9. Major Charles S. Severson was chief quartermaster with General Forrest in January, 1864.

10. Apparently the Wilson property lay in both Marshall and DeSoto counties.

11. April 6-7, 1862.

12. Dr. Wilson refers to the Conscription Act, passed April 16, 1862, which drafted able-bodied men between eighteen and thirty-five

for three years or the war. A major purpose was the stimulation of volunteering on the part of those whose twelve months' service would soon expire.

13. Brigadier General James Ronald Chalmers, former Holly Springs lawyer and district attorney, fought in the battle of Shiloh. Later transferred to the cavalry, he was in command of a force of that branch or the last two years of the war. At the surrender he was the commander of the First Division of Forrest's Army Corps.

14. Robert W. Locke was mustered out at Grand Junction, Tennessee, on March 31, 1862, with the same general purpose in mind.

## CHAPTER XIV

1. This was Company D, 42nd Mississippi Regiment. The regiment was organized May 14, 1862 in Oxford and moved to Grenada on June 12. Of 82 men rolled, 16 were killed or died of wounds, three were discharged, eight transferred, and eight deserted.

2. Locke was Wilson's close friend from Thyatira. At Buck Snort Locke received 28 votes to 15 for Wilson as captain of Company D. Locke was seriously wounded at Gettysburg and was absent on leave for a good part of the rest of the war. He achieved his majority on December 18, 1863.

3. See Chapter XXI, footnote 3.

4. Lieutenant Jones died of wounds incurred at Bristoe Station.

5. Sergeant J. M. Atkins was killed at Gettysburg.

6. The companies of the 42nd Mississippi Regiment were listed as follows: A (Carroll Fencibles), Captain Andrew M. Nelson; B (Senatobia Invincibles), Captain William A. Feeney; C (Nelm's Avengers), Captain W. P. Smith; D, Captain Robert W. Locke; E (Davenport Rifles), Captain Henry Davenport; F, Captain Thomas G. Clark (killed at Gettysburg); G (Gaston Rifles), Captain James M. Gaston (killed at Gettysburg); H, Captain Jeff J. Meek (resigned, 1863), Captain Robert M. Buchanan; K, Captain Goldsborough B. Mears (killed at Gettysburg).

Most of the records of the 42nd Mississippi Regiment have long since faded into illegibility. Following is exact copy of a partial roster:

| Name | Rank | Age |
|---|---|---|
| Adkins, J. M. | 1st Sgt. | 25 |
| Burford, M. N. | Corporal | 25 |
| Eavanson, J. M. | Private | 33 |
| Finley, John T. | Private | 26 |
| Galloway, Wm. T. | Private | 27 |
| Gossett, Wm. | Private | 17 |
| Haines, Thos. J. | Private | 20 |
| Howze, Geo. A. | 2nd Lt. | 30 |
| King, Jas. R. | Private | 28 |

| Name | Rank | Age |
|---|---|---|
| Lawson, John | Private | 39 |
| Morgan, Lafayette | Sgt. | 35 |
| McClain, J. M. | Private | 28 |
| Norfleet, Albert A. | Private | 16 |
| Perry, George | Private | 28 |
| Smith, David | Private | 26 |
| Smith, M. H. | Sergeant | 21 |
| White, Robert M. | Private | 19 |
| Jones, M. J. | Lieut. | |
| White, R. F. | Private | |
| Yocum, D. C. | Private | |
| Wall, M. H. | Private | |
| Kersey, R. I. | Private | |
| Cannon, W. H. | Private | |
| Minor, I. P. | Private | |

| Place | Died |
|---|---|
| killed Gettysburg | July 1, 1863 |
| Point Lookout | Dec. 1, 1863 |
| pneumonia Richmond | Oct. 28, 1862 |
| Hospital | Nov. 15, 1862 |
| fever near Richmond | Sept. 7, 1862 |
| near Richmond | Oct. 12, 1862 |
| near Richmond | Oct. 2, 1862 |
| killed Gettysburg | July 1, 1863 |
| hospital Richmond | Nov. 17, 1862 |
| Pa. wounded Gettysburg | Sept. 15, 1863 |
| killed Gettysburg | July 1, 1863 |
| Point Lookout | Jan. 1, 1864 |
| (discharged Feb. 4, 1864) | |
| North Carolina | Aug. 30, 1862 |
| near Richmond | Nov. 15, 1862 |
| Point Lookout | Dec. 26, 1863 |
| wounded Gettysburg | Oct. 15, 1863 |
| gen. hospital Richmond | June 3, 1864 |
| (date, place death not given) | |
| killed Spotsylvania | May 12, 1864 |
| disease pris. of war | Aug. 1, 1864 |
| wounds Petersburg | Sept. 4, 1864 |
| disease pris. of war | Aug. 1, 1864 |
| disease Petersburg | Aug. 11, 1864 |

7.  Colonel Hugh R. Miller moved about 1840 to Pontotoc, where he became a circuit judge. He organized a company in Pontotoc in 1861 and went directly to Virginia. In command of a brigade, he was killed at Gettysburg. See Chapter XXI, footnote 15.

8.  From Panola County, Dr. Hillery Moseley was crippled at Gettysburg. See Chapter XXI, footnote 15.

9.  Major Feeney, from Senatobia, was wounded at Gettysburg and killed in the Wilderness. See Chapter XXVI, footnote 1; Chapter XX, footnote 3, and Chapter XXIX, footnote 2.

10. Benjamin F. Jones, close friend of Wilson, is mentioned often in both the Wilson and Locke narratives. See Chapter XVIII, footnote 6; Chapter XIX, footnotes 5, 6; and Chapter XXI, footnote 12.

11. Dr. Marion J. Rossel was surgeon of Company C. See Chapter XVII.

12. Robert L. Taggart was assistant-surgeon of Company F. See Chapter XVII.

13. Adjutant Oliver S. Carr was wounded in the Wilderness.

14. This trip illustrates the inconvenience of travel in the Confederacy. As there was no through and direct rail connection between Meridian and Montgomery, the rivers were used. The regiment left for Richmond on June 22, arrived in Mobile on the 25th, whence the men traveled to Montgomery by boat and train. In Montgomery, Dr. Wilson became sick, stayed at the Exchange Hotel overnight for $3.00, and then moved into a private residence for six days (at $1.50 per day). On July 5 Wilson and Captain Locke left for Richmond where they arrived at Camp Lee and "slept on corn sacks—bad night of it."

15. The Seven Days Battle took place June 26-July 2, 1862. The 42d Regiment arrived in Richmond on July 3.

16. The gunboats rendered General McClellan efficient service in the battle of Malvern Hill but hardly saved his army from "utter annihilation."

17. Previously known as the Fair Grounds. Public executions as well as parades took place at Camp Lee during the war. In September, Captain Locke wrote in his diary: "I saw two Irishmen shot for desertion. It was a tragedy I had not seen before—also saw man whipped 50 lashes with a strap on his nakedness."

18. On February 25, 1863, Captain Locke wrote that Norfleet was "fresh from home" with many letters.

19. Both Norfleet and Carmichael were privates in Company D, 42nd Mississippi Regiment.

## CHAPTER XV

1. This was in September, 1862. According to Clifford Dowdey: "Belle Island was a beautiful green island in the James River. Slopes rose from the water to a low hill, and around the banks of foliage the water rippled in eddies and falls. A favorite spot for Richmonders before the war, it was ideally situated as a prison. It was outside the overcrowded city proper, the rapids of the river made escape difficult (some prisoners were drowned trying), and the hill made it possible for a few guards with obsolete cannons to control the thousands below. But for living conditions, with the acute shortage of everything in the South, the island became a horror for the men."

2. See Chapter XXI, footnote 15.

3. General Pope's order of July 14, 1862, stated: "I have come to you from the West, where we have always seen the backs of our enemies, from an army whose business it has been to seek the adversary, and to beat him when he was found; whose policy has been attack and not defense. . . . I desire you to dismiss from your minds certain phrases, which I am sorry to find so much in vogue among you. I hear constantly of 'taking strong positions and holding them,' of 'lines of retreat' and of 'bases of supplies.' Let us discard such ideas. . . . Let us study the probable lines of retreat of our opponents, and leave our own to take care of themselves. . . ."

4. August 9, 1862.

5. August 26, 1862.

6. August 29-30, 1862.

7. Robert Selph Henry has stated: "On the seventeenth day of September in 1862 the decline of the Confederacy began."

## CHAPTER XVI

1. General George B. McClellan.

2. The 42nd Mississippi Regiment was ordered to Fredericksburg on November 15, 1862 and returned to Richmond exactly one week later (the day the Union army started towards Fredericksburg).

3. November 17, 1862. Captain Locke recorded the bantering that went on between Yanks and Rebs across the river. When the Yankees criticized the southern uniforms, Tom Martin replied, "You are a set of damned fools. Do you suppose we put on our good clothes to go out to kill damn dogs in?"

4. Andrew M. Nelson, 31 year old lawyer from Carrollton, was captain of Company A of the 42nd Mississippi Regiment. He was promoted to lieutenant colonel July 17, 1863. Seriously wounded in the Wilderness, he was absent on leave for several months. After the war he was private secretary to Governor John M. Stone and Adjutant General of the Mississippi state troops. See Chapter XXXI, footnote 2.

5. Captain Locke wrote: "I must say in justice to the ladies of Fredericksburg that many ladies have done well but they surpassed them all—such hospitality to soldiers, devotion to the interests of the South, zeal amounting to enthusiasm in the cause of the Confederacy I am certain has never been excelled."

6. On May 17, 1863, "Lt. Howze and Captain Powell were baptized." See Chapter XXVIII, footnote 1, Chapter XXX, footnote 11.

7. In January, 1863 the 42nd Regiment "got up a subscription" for the relief of the citizens of Fredericksburg. Captain Locke made the following record: "Company A, 80 men, $100; Company B, 60

men, $110; Company C, 80 men, $60; Company D, 60 men, $140; Company E, 32 men, $50; Company F, 100 men, $40; Company G, 90 men, $23; Company H, 90 men, $114; Company I, 80 men, $15. Total, $652."

## CHAPTER XVII

1. See Chapter XIV, footnote 12.

2. Captain Locke reported that "Lt. Wilson is a little wrathy. about the way Col. Miller treated him with reference to his appointment to the asst. Surgency of the Regt. & I don't blame him for he has been treated badly."

3. According to Locke there was "Some interest in the Co. about the election of a Lt. to fill the vacancy made by Dr. Wilson's promotion to captain."

4. The 42nd was ordered south of the James River on December 13, 1862. Six or eight miles below Richmond, on the river, were the Confederate batteries at Drewry's Bluff.

## CHAPTER XVIII

1. Actually, Burnsides' campaign to Richmond via Fredericksburg got underway about the middle of November. The story told here is essentially correct. Under protection of artillery placed on Stafford Heights, some 76,000 Federals crossed the Rappahannock on the night of December 11. On the 13th they were severely repulsed and two days later withdrew across the river. In the battle of Fredericksburg the Union army lost 12,653 dead and wounded compared to Lee's loss of 5,309.

2. In January, 1863, the 42nd was composed of ten companies, as follows: Company A, Captain A. M. Nelson; Company B, Captain, S. G. Woollard; Company C, Captain W. P. Smith; Company D, Captain Locke (Lieutenants Wilson, M. J. Jones, and George A. Howze) ; Company E, Captain Davenport; Company F, Captain Clark; Company G, Captain Gaston; Company H, Captain John Powell; Company J, Captain Jeff Meek; Company K, Captain Mears.

3. On February 1 Locke made a settlement with Wilson and Howze—"eatables cost 24-79/100 dollars, negro hire 32-29/100 dollars." Lt. Howze planned to visit Mississippi—"has had a chicken cooked for several days to carry with him,"—but was turned down.

4. The 42nd Regiment was ordered to Goldsboro on December 15, 1862, arrived on the 17th when it took its place in line of battle on the Neuse River. On January 7, 1863, according to Locke, "Dr. Wilson and our sick left at camp came up with our baggage & we

again had tents." (Captain Locke was told by Lieutenant Howze "that Goldsboro is a bad place for 'lewd women of the basest sort,' he has met them on patrol.")

Some 15,000 Confederate soldiers under General Longstreet spent the winter of 1862-1863 in southeastern Virginia and eastern North Carolina. These troops did not participate in the battle of Chancellorsville.

5. The 42nd Regiment was engaged at this time in some skirmishing. Locke reported in January, 1863: "Dr. Wilson is going to mess with Captain Jones, for his accommodation I suppose as he has a negro and Jones has none."

6. See Chapter XIV, footnote 10; Chapter XVIII, footnote 6; Chapter XXI, footnote 12. The tax-in-kind, or Tithe Tax, was authorized by the Confederate Congress on April 24, 1863. Every farmer was compelled to pay one-tenth of his produce as a tax-in-kind.

7. The 42nd Regiment returned to Richmond on June 22, 1863, and one week later was sent to Fredericksburg.

8. Davis' Brigade, the 4th Brigade of Henry Heth's Division, 3rd Army Corps, under General A. P. Hill, was composed of the 2nd Mississippi (Colonel J. M. Stone), 11th Mississippi (Colonel F. M. Greene), 42nd Mississippi (Colonel Hugh R. Miller), and the 55th North Carolina (Colonel J. K. Connally).

9. Henry Heth, native Virginian, West Point graduate and Mexican War veteran, had been a division commander in General Bragg's Kentucky invasion and later commanded the Department of East Tennessee. He took part in the battles of Chancellorsville and Gettysburg and surrendered with General Lee at Appomattox.

10. In the reorganization of the Confederate Army after the death of General Jackson, Ambrose P. Hill was made lieutenant general and given command of Lee's 3rd Army Corps.

11. At this time Company D listed the following non-commissioned officers: J. M. Adkins, 1st Sgt.; Philomon White, 2nd Sgt.; W. H. Smith, 3rd Sgt.; George R. Yocom, 4th Sgt.; W. L. Hancock, 5th Sgt.; Lafayette Morgan, 1st Corp.; John G. Anderson, 2nd Corp.; R. E. Cason, 3rd Corp.; Whit Carter, 4th Corp.

## CHAPTER XIX

1. On June 6, according to Locke's diary, "Dr. Wilson and I took a long walk up to the high range of hills that overlook the old city—nothing but ruin and desolation to be seen."

2. The one-legged Lieutenant General Ewell was given command of Jackson's II Corps after Chancellorsville. Dr. Wilson's statements in this paragraph are quite accurate.

3. Before the 42nd pulled out for the invasion of Pennsylvania, there had been formed in the regiment a Christian Association, with Major Feeney as permanent president, Lieutenant Howze as permanent secretary, and Chaplain Witherspoon as corresponding secretary.

4. On June 27 Captain Locke wrote in his diary: "We hear the Yanks have 200,000 Militia & 100,000 Regulars concentrated to head us off. We may have bad times yet before we reach Washington City but I still hope to get back to Dixie. If the Yankees put forth all their strength the chance is slim but our trust is in the God of battles & our own strong arms."

5. For Thomas Dwight Witherspoon, see Chapter XXV.

## CHAPTER XX

1. This "brooklet" was Willoughby's Run, which did cross diagonally the field where the battle of Gettysburg began.

2. On this day the 42nd Regiment was on the right of the Confederate battle line, in the fight for possession of the hills west of Gettysburg. Moseley and Feeney were severely wounded. The 42nd took about 150 prisoners.

3. George Adrian Howze, son of Dr. Wilson's sister, Elizabeth James Wilson Howze, married Mollie White of Murfreesboro, Tenn., in December, 1859. They commenced housekeeping in Memphis in 1860. As mentioned on page 86, Lt. Howze enlisted in the 42nd Mississippi Regiment and reached Richmond in June, 1862. In Eldon Roark's column in the Memphis *Press-Scimitar* (April 29, May 2, 1953) are several excerpts from the diary of Lieutenant Howze, who had moved from Marshall County, Miss., to Memphis in 1858 to take a position in a large wholesale house at $700 per year.

Howze's diary illustrates both the temptations of Memphis and the state of the young man's mind: " 'Take care, young man,' still continued to intrude itself upon me ever and anon, and I felt it was but the voice of God speaking to me. Temptation was around me in a thousand forms. On every corner of the street the monster stood, clothed in the soft habiliments of a friend."

Some of Howze's associates "were in the habit of going to the saloon 2 or 3 times a day. The theater was another temptation. I attended this place of public amusement and did not think it a great sin to go to a moderate extent. 'Richard,' 'Romeo and Juliet,' 'Merchant of Venice,' 'Hidden Hand,' were all plays which I felt upon me had a most glorious effect, and I went frequently."

"Another fearful vice and temptation in a city is a house of bad repute, and I thank God in one of these I have never entered."

"There is the billiard saloon, the 10 pin alley, gaming table, keeping bad company, etc. In none of these things did I indulge. My trust was in God to keep me from it."

The diary of Lt. Howze ended on May 12, 1863, when his regiment was near Ivor, Virginia. At that time, just after Chancellorsville, things were rather quiet, and the young soldier had filled all the pages of his book.

The faithful servant, Stephen made a rude coffin for his master, whose body was later removed to Hollywood cemetery in Richmond. Lt. Howze left an infant son Arthur, who graduated from the United' States Naval Academy and later died of typhoid fever.

Captain Locke gives a fine description of the first day's fighting at Gettysburg. Sergeant Adkins was killed and Locke was struck in the side by a piece of shell. As he fell to the ground "Lt. Howze, who was an amiable gentleman, came up & desired to know if I was hurt & said to me to 'take care of myself,' & raised up and started off. The Regt. was then falling back, he had gone but a few steps when he fell dead. His health was too feeble to have been in the field, but it was his first fight & he was a man of great pride of character & was determined to do nothing that might tarnish his honorable reputation."

4. Captain Locke wrote that "of the 45 boys I took into the fight 25 were killed or wounded."

5. General Heth was wounded early in the battle. General James J. Pettigrew took over the division which was one of three taking part in Pickett's charge. From Mississippi the 2nd, 11th, and 42nd participated. The 42nd Mississippi lost 32 killed and 170 wounded in the charge and 62 killed (plus 13 who died as prisoners after the battle) in the whole Gettysburg campaign. Captain Locke could find only eight men from Company D—"our Rgt. literally cut to pieces."

6. Jeremiah Gage was a sergeant in Company A of the 11th Mississippi Regiment. He wrote to his mother: "My dear Mother, This is the last you may ever hear from me. I have time to tell you that I died like a man. Bear my loss the best you can. Remember that I am true to my country and that my greatest regret at dying is that she is not free and that you and my sisters are robbed of my worth whatever that may be. . . ."

7. Instead of July 6th, as reported by the author, Gen. Imboden's wagon train of wounded left Gettysburg on the afternoon of July 4th and reached Williamsport in the late afternoon of the 5th.

8. Captain Locke wrote: "The enemy attacked our train at different times but our cavalry, Gen. Imboden, drove them off."

9. General Imboden's independent brigade of 2,100 cavalry took no part in the battle of Gettysburg. He was ordered by Lee to escort the wounded back to Virginia. His train was seventeen miles long when put into motion. He wrote:

"I was never out of hearing of the groans and cries of the wounded and dying. Scarcely one in a hundred had received adequate surgical aid, owing to the demands on the hard-working surgeons from still worse cases that had to be left behind. Many of the wounded in the wagons had been without food for thirty-six hours. Their torn and bloody clothing, matted and hardened, was rasping the tender, inflamed, and still oozing wounds. Very few of the wagons had even a layer of straw in them, and all were without springs. The road was rough and rocky from the heavy washings of the preceding day. . . .

"Some were simply moaning; some were praying, and others uttering the most fearful oaths and execrations that despair and agony could wring from them; while a majority, with a stoicism sustained by sublime devotion to the cause they fought for, endured without complaint unspeakable tortures, and even spoke words of cheer and comfort to their unhappy comrades. . . . During this one night I realized more of the horrors of war than I had in all the two preceding years."

10.   For additional detail on the retreat from Gettysburg, with special reference to the train of wounded see General Imboden's vivid account in *Battles and Leaders*, III, 420-429.

11.   "The Wagoners Battle" took place on July 6th. About seven hundred wagoners, organized in companies of 100 each, fought magnificently in throwing back a heavy Federal attack.

12.   See Chapter XIV, footnote 10 and Chapter XIX, footnote 6.

13.   In his diary Captain Locke wrote that in the Gettysburg fight his company had lost three killed, 25 wounded, and ten missing. Among the wounded he listed:

"John P. English, shot in leg; George M. Eavenson, leg and head, flesh; James M. Farmer, arm, flesh; L. P. Hancock, arm; W. L. Hancock, leg off near the knee; E. W. Ingram, shoulder; L. Ingram, leg off above the knee; Luke Johnson, leg, flesh; Wm. L. Kerr, hand; R. J. Kersey, leg, flesh, contusion; F. R. King, finger & captured; W. A. McCall, arm broken, serious; J. H. Mc——, through the abdomen, serious; C. W. Ruby (?), leg off below knee; Jacob Sansom, arm broken, serious; Henderson Sorrell, slight, in head; Willis C. Sullivan, head, serious; John Pinkney Thompson, in foot, prisoner; Perry H. Walker, knee joint, serious; H. M. Wall, slight, in leg; R. M. White, arm broken, died; W. F. Wilson, face, left eye shot out."

14.   Maggots in wounds may well have saved many lives. Dr. Wilson was unaware, of course, of maggot therapy which has been described as "Treatment of infected wounds and draining sinuses, as in osteomyelitis, by means of blowfly maggots, which prevent suppuration by killing bacteria and dissolving necrotic tissues with proteolytic enzymes, leaving living tissues uninjured."

15.   The Captain in command was A. M. Nelson, who at Cold Harbor (see p.177) was still regimental commander. He was promoted

to colonel later. The dead colonel was Hugh Miller, the crippled lieutenant colonel, Hillery Moseley, and the wounded major, William Feeney. The Fourth Brigade (2nd, 115th, 42nd Mississippi and 55th North Carolina) lost 180 killed, 717 wounded.

## CHAPTER XXII

1. By August, 1863 this was the only practicable method of corresponding with the folks at home.

2. The chances are that Dr. Wilson boarded the Mobile and Ohio train at Meridian after a ride from Selma on the Alabama and Mississippi Railroad, although he may have traveled from Montgomery to Mobile either by steamship or by the Alabama and Florida and the Mobile and Great Northern Railroads.

3. Captain Locke arrived home on August 2: "Great many neighbors and friends came in. They had heard nothing reliable from friends in Gettysburg fight. I had sad news for many of them. Mrs. Howze especially excited my commisseration." On September 6 he wrote: "Hear Dr. Wilson has got home."

4. According to Dr. Wilson, the Negroes were faithful and would save stock from raiders. "A raid would start from Memphis. As soon as the people learned the road it would take, a horn would blow and it would be taken up and down the line of that road and in thirty minutes the people would be warned for thirty miles. This gave the people time to hide their provisions and stock."

5. Wilson left home in company with Captain Locke and James Crawford. Three days later they had gotten to Meridian. At Selma each paid four dollars for supper and bed. At midnight, October 7, they left for Montgomery on boat, "Rober B. Taney." Train connections from Montgomery were excellent, the group traveling via West Point, Atlanta, Augusta, Kingsville, Columbia, Charlotte, and Raleigh. On the 12th Dr. Wilson stopped in Petersburg at the home of his uncle, Adrian Bourdon.

6. At Bristoe Station, October 14, 1863, the 42nd lost six killed, twenty-five wounded. Apparently, Captain Locke returned on October 23rd to his company which was then stationed at Brandy Station. He was "glad to see the boys." On the next day he paid his respects to General Davis and "Dr. Wilson and I went to the 19th Miss., saw Lt. Col. Hardin, came back & went on picket." On November 8, his company was called out at three in the morning, took a battle position, engaged in skirmishing, and marched all night to the Rapidan. Crossing the river, Company D settled down for the winter in "Camp Freeze Out."

7. Captain Locke wrote on November 24: "Finished our hut & Captain. Wilson loaned me his fly tent & I am somewhat comfortable again but not well." A week later Locke was in a Richmond hospital carrying on an extended correspondence with Dr. Wilson on the subject of his possible resignation. On December 18 he was back in camp— "Dr. Wilson had an ambulance waiting for me." On the 20th: "Dr. Wilson, my particular friend, has written out my application for 60 days leave." Two days later he bade goodbye to Company D. "It is composed of noble men (with one infamous exception, John Moore)." Locke was appointed major on December 18, 1863.

It is apparent from Locke's diary that during the winter months Dr. Wilson requested a transfer to Mississippi, where he was assured of appointment as surgeon to Colonel McQuirk's 3rd Mississippi Cavalry. The transfer was not made, probably because McQuirk's muster rolls were not on file in the Adjutant General's Office and the 3rd Mississippi Cavalry could not be officially recognized as in the Confederate service. According to the Surgeon General the "rolls of the western troops were in a jumble."

## CHAPTER XXIII

1. Chaplain General J. William Jones spoke of Thomas D. Witherspoon as "one of the most devoted, untiring, self sacrificing, and efficient chaplains that we had in the army. The Reverend Mr. Witherspoon was born in Greensboro, Alabama, on January 17, 1836 and died in Louisville, Kentucky, in November, 1898. A graduate of the class of 1856 at the University of Mississippi, Witherspoon studied under Dr. Thornwell at the Presbyterian Seminary in Columbia, S. C., and was ordained May 23, 1860. His first pastorate was in Oxford, Miss., from which he entered the Lamar Rifles as a private. Later he became chaplain of the 2nd Mississippi Infantry, and then of the 42nd Mississippi Regiment upon its formation in 1862. After the war, Witherspoon held pastorates in Memphis, Petersburg, and Louisville, and at his death was professor of homiletics and pastoral theology at the Presbyterian Seminary in Louisville.

2. On February 8, 1863, Captain Locke recorded: "Chaplain Witherspoon preached in camp. He said the Lord had brought this season to chastize us & when we were humbled we would have peace, etc."

## CHAPTER XXIV

1. In January, 1863, Captain Locke wrote in his diary: "Dr. McReight and Lt. Wilson played a long game of chess in my tent,

Major Feeney looking on trying to learn the game." Hardly in the category of winter amusement was a petition signed by sixteen officers of the 42nd Regiment (including "L. J. Wilson, Capt. and Asst. Surgeon") requesting Captain A. M. Nelson and Captain W. P. Smith to waive the question of rank in favor of Captain Locke. Nelson turned down the petition.

2. Or clappers. Short strips of bone, ivory, or wood, held in pairs between the fingers and used to mark time or produce musical rhythms.

## CHAPTER XXV

1. According to Robert Selph Henry: "There were marches and counter-marches of the two armies in Virginia in October, when Lee's threatened advance toward Washington caused Meade to fall back all the way to Centreville, where the Confederates had spent the first winter of the war; and again in November, when Meade's threatening advance across the Rappahannock and the Rapidan brought Lee into line of battle along Mine Run, where, during the last days of the month, the armies bristled toward each other until, on December first, Meade withdrew from what appeared to be an unprofitable undertaking, and went into winter quarters between the Rapidan and the Rappahannock."

## CHAPTER XXVI

1. See Chapter XVI, footnote 6; Chapter XXXI, footnote 11.
2. Gath was famous as the birthplace of Goliath. "Tell it not in Gath, publish it not in the streets of Askelon; lest the daughters of the Philistines rejoice, lest the daughters of the uncircumcised triumph." 2 Samuel, I, 20.

## CHAPTER XXVII

1. Probably Samuel Walker, 48th Mississippi Regiment, who was killed at Hatcher's run.

## CHAPTER XXVIII

1. Estimates of General Grant's available troops run from 117,000 to 127,000. In all General Lee could assemble between 61,000 and 65,000 men.
2. Major Feeney is frequently mentioned in the Locke diary. See Chapter XIV, footnote 9; Chapter XXVI, footnote 1.

3. Surgeon of Stonewall Jackson's Corps, Dr. McGuire was with Jackson at his death.

4. This, of course, is a famous incident, retold with all its dramatic impact in volume III of Freeman's *R. E. Lee.*

5. During May 5-7, 1864, General Grant's losses were 17,666 while those of General Lee came to approximately 7,600.

6. These figures are correct. Dr. Wilson apparently did considerable checking before he made estimates of battle losses.

7. In the May campaign, the 42nd Mississippi Regiment lost 15 killed, 95 wounded, nine missing.

8. Hancock is buried in little family cemetery just west of Wall Hill. The tombstone has on it the phrase "A gallant Confederate Soldier." The 19th Mississippi Regiment was commanded by Colonel Thomas J. Hardin, "doubly connected with the [Wilson] family by marriage." He fell at the bloody angle of Spotsylvania.

## CHAPTER XXIX

1. William Swinton, *Campaigns of the Army of the Potomac* (1866).

2. As late as February, 1865, Colonel Nelson was in command of the brigade and General Davis of the division. See Chapter XVI, footnote 4.

3. Actually, General Grant did not at first ask permission to remove the wounded who lay on the field of Cold Harbor from June 4 to the evening of June 7.

4. General Ben Butler was "corked in a battle" by General Beauregard at Bermuda Hundred.

5. Dr. Wilson writes very little about himself in this period. Major Locke reported on June 11, 1864 that he had been informed by the Surgeon General that Wilson "would be promoted if he was the senior assistant of his corps."

6. The Union loss at the Crater was somewhat below 4,000 casualties.

7. James Redpath was a newspaper correspondent with the northern armies during the war.

8. August 18, 1864. Dr. Wilson is correct in his figures.

9. Of the 965 men on the roll of the 42nd Mississippi Regiment, 139 died of disease, and 143 were killed or died of wounds.

10. The 42nd Regiment lost eight wounded and missing at Jones' Farm, October 23, 1864, and was later engaged at Hatcher's Run.

11. On June 20, 1864, according to Locke's diary, Powell was brought to a Richmond hospital, badly wounded in the thigh. Major

Locke himself was hospitalized in Mississippi, although as late as December 6, 1864, his resignation papers were still to be approved.

12. John William Jones, *School History of the United States* (1896). Jones also wrote *Personal Reminiscences, Anecdotes, and Letters of Gen. Robert E. Lee* (1874), *Life and Letters of Robert Edward Lee* (1906), and *Christ in The Camp* (1887).

13. When the Petersburg line was broken, the colors of the 42nd Mississippi Regiment were captured on April 2, 1865 by the 11th Vermont Regiment.

14. According to Colonel Charles S. Venable, Lee's words were: "Then there is nothing left me to do but to go and see General Grant, and I would rather die a thousand deaths."

15. With the slight changes noted in the text, Dr. Wilson has General Orders No. 9 correct, except that in the original there were four paragraphs.